John,

To the highest but best shooter
I know, who has Kindled my
desire to hunt and who will
hopefully be my blind-mate (?)
for years to come.

With love & affection;

Slim

DAYS AFIELD

Drawings by Jennifer Dewey

E. P. DUTTON, INC. | NEW YORK

DAYS AFIELD

Journeys and Discoveries in Hunting and Fishing

Thomas McIntyre

Foreword by Tom Paugh, Editor, *Sports Afield*

Published in the United States by
E. P. Dutton, Inc.,
2 Park Avenue, New York, N.Y. 10016

Library of Congress Cataloging in Publication Data
McIntyre, Thomas.
Days afield
1. Hunting—North America. 2. Fishing—North America.
I. Title.
SK40.M36   1984   799'.097   83-20614

ISBN: 0-525-24227-9

Published simultaneously in Canada
by Fitzhenry and Whiteside
Limited, Toronto

Designed by Mark O'Connor

10 9 8 7 6 5 4 3 2 1

First Edition

For my mother and my father

Contents

Foreword

For a writer, Thomas McIntyre is a big guy. He has a voice big enough to match his girth and a personality of sufficient force to dominate a room. (Make that a large room.) And he has wit. It is always an entertaining experience to spend some time in his company. But that is not the half of it.

The more—much more—than 50 percent of it is that Tom McIntyre is a writer all the way. I'm sure that it has never occurred to him to be anything else. In this technological era there is something reassuring about a young man dedicating his life to laboriously placing words on paper one at a time in the age-old way.

Something more: Tom McIntyre is an outdoorsman. This means that he hunts, camps, fishes, and participates in activities that not only link humans to nature but also connect present-day man to his heritage, another reassuring fact in a world very much preoccupied with its own total destruction. While in certain circles it is now considered fashionable to malign sportsmen for killing "helpless" animals, the stark facts are that today's hunters and anglers are at the forefront of the conservation movement to preserve breeding territories, wild waters, and open spaces.

Goliath (encroaching civilization, industrial pollution, and runaway population growth) likes to pick on David (the sportsmen of the world), blaming him for atrocities against nature. Tom McIntyre knows the truth of the matter and knows how to write about it.

He does not dwell on the negatives. Rather it is the fun of being afield that comes through in these essays, the enrichment and the soul-stirring pleasures that belong to those of us who seek adventure in the great outdoors.

I had occasion recently to ask Tom why he had become a writer about things outdoors. He told me, in part: "I write, first of all, because it is what I do. I have succeeded in learning no other craft, so for better or worse a writer is what I am bound to be. Then there is this fierce, sometimes almost ludicrous passion I feel for the wild and being at large with rod and gun. Put these two together and what you have on your hands is an outdoor writer."

That doesn't quite explain why he is an outdoor writer of another level. I spend my days (and nights and weekends) reading the work of writers in this field. Frankly, outdoor writing has seldom been considered at the apex of literary endeavor. My aching eyes have seen much to support that position. At *Sports Afield* we strive mightily to discover and encourage the best of the best, and some readers have been kind enough to tell us we are succeeding. If we are, it is because of Thomas McIntyre and a few (very few) of his peers. My eyes do not ache when I read a McIntyre manuscript. They light up.

Why is his writing on another level? He told me: "I would like to believe that my work has at least a fighting chance of achieving some manner of permanence. I cannot say it actually will, nor can I say if it is possible for outdoor writing ever to cross over that all too vague line into what we deem art."

There we have the primary clue to the secret of the man and his words. He isn't writing just to pay the electric bill. Words that are aimed at posterity have to be carefully chosen. The words of Thomas McIntyre are right on target. This book represents the first step of this author in the direction of "permanence." I have the feeling that someday the "McIntyre library" will contain a significant number of volumes.

I have not really studied enough forewords to remember if I am supposed to tell you such things as: Thomas Alfred McIntyre was born at 3:10 P.M., January 23, 1952, in Downey, California; was educated at a Sisters of Notre Dame parochial school, Loyola High School (Los Angeles), and attended (three years) Reed College in Portland, Oregon, before leaving because he had (in his words) "no friends left among the faculty in the English Department." If these were the kinds of facts you were looking for, I apologize.

What I have tried instead to give you is some slight insight into what makes Thomas McIntyre tick as a writer. Perhaps the key word I have been searching for is *drive.* Tom is committed to achieving what he knows deep inside he was born to do, and he has all the tools necessary: talent, a rich sense of history, technical expertise, a hearty streak of humor, and—drive.

If the question is, will Thomas McIntyre make it to the top of the outdoor writing heap, then the answer resides in this book, *Days Afield.* He not only will make it, he has arrived.

TOM PAUGH, EDITOR,
Sports Afield

Preface

The river comes from a lake. It flows in a singular green clarity through canyons of spruce, jack pine, and poplar, past gravel bars made up of rounded gray stones and of cottonwoods one jump ahead of beaver, before joining with other rivers—opaque blue ones out of glaciers—and reaching at last an ocean. Along it are to be seen mature and immature eagles, humped blond grizzly, more mosquitoes than absolutely called for, and as I write these words a king salmon up from the sea breaks from the deep water of a pool far below me and hurtles back in. After everything else, though, it remains a river. It is by no means a metaphor.

I have written some tales, for the most part true, and if they succeed at all there will be seen to be a flow to them as well. As far as I can tell, however, they are not metaphors for anything either.

They begin in the Far West of North America, in its game fields and water and hills, because that is where my beginnings are and to its game fields and water and hills I was drawn at an age when I was much too young to speculate widely concerning reasons why. That came later, and these stories are in part an unavoidable outgrowth of such speculation.

Though a Westerner—or rather that most extreme realization of the phenomenon, a *Californian*—by accident of birth, I remain one by choice, as I have, again by choice, remained a hunter and a fisher. Since the West no longer requires our "winning" and game has come to be viewed by some in a, let us say, *different* light, there seems to be little call these days for our being any of the above, but for that very reason the decision to be any and all of them is made just a bit more consequential. For myself it is a decision by which I will simply have to stand.

In being drawn into the current that I was (and this has led me, as it would, to places somewhat beyond the Far West), I have seen some things. Among them have been wild pigeons in a gyre in the air; dove flighting to seed crops at evening; hounds bawling; trout rising; ducks flaring; a gobbler on the strut; bull elk on the run; bear big as all outdoors laying specific claim to a stretch of trail or riverbank; Cape buffalo bigger yet, announcing: Dont Tread on Me; and the native bison of this continent, still looking biggest of all and needing to make no announcements whatsoever. These, and lakes and streams and marshes and lagoons, a few gradients timbered and above timber, a certain amount of wind and sun and rain and night and stars and moon, some death, but on the whole a good deal more life, are what I have seen in the places I have been in following that current. While many, if not most, of you have no doubt seen some of them better than I, my wish is to try to tell you how it was for me to see them, sometimes for the first time.

What I have not done in these tales, I hope, is carry on about the passing away of the hunter and fisher's "way of life." My personal conviction is that, one way or another, such a life will always be possible, and needed to be led. The want to *know* wild animals and wild land, to function within that special realm, is inside us all, whether we actively engage in the effort or not, whether we even admit to it or not. You and I—if you are reading these words and not studying this book curiously as some odd found object you will carry back to camp and display to the rest of your clan, unfamiliar with the printed page because you have been wise enough to maintain your tradition of story-telling—you and I may no longer pursue game out of an unqualified necessity to feed our stomachs, but we do it to slake other less domitable hungers, hungers truly ancient. Our getting up and going out *is* as old as those hills, and we are likely to continue in the practice for quite some time to come. It also helps that we do seem to enjoy it so.

Like that river, a flow is continuous. The circle of rain to lake to river to ocean to air to rain again is far too elementary and unbroken to warrant exposition at this time. The rudiments of our lives alter, certainly; but pass away? Hardly. Even as it moves by, this river returns. And we do appear to be drifting parlously near metaphor here.

What all this comes down to finally is my hope that you will be able to take some pleasure in these tales. They arise out of happy times in places that generally persist in being unruly and disinclined to pass away. Such places have always been, at least for me, genuine sights for sore eyes. Perhaps, along the way yourself, you may see something in them too. I hope you'll have a look.

NAKINA RIVER,   T.M.
NORTHWEST BRITISH COLUMBIA   JULY 1983

DAYS AFIELD

The Bandtail Above All

> *. . . the pursuer cannot pursue if he does not integrate his vision with that of the pursued. That is to say,* hunting is an imitation of the animal.
>
> —JOSÉ ORTEGA Y GASSET,
> "MEDITATIONS ON HUNTING"

Our proper pursuits vary greatly. They are, in that highly vaunted final analysis, whatever *means* something to us. I do not know what yours are, but mine begin with something as simple as a bird, a bandtail pigeon. Yet on second thought, there is nothing really very simple about pursuing a bandtail.

Please do not confuse the bandtail, by the way, with those pigeons who infest cities. The bright lights hold no allure for the bandtail. That creature you see puffing lickerishly in parks and strutting arrogantly on the ledges of office windows is a rock dove, a refugee from the Old World, where—in Iraq, for example—he has been a domesticated animal since 4500 B.C. He has now simply gone feral and is a common hooligan and jackanapes to boot—host to enough diseases to require a warning label.

Bandtails are authentically Pacific Coast birds, and when you see vast flights of them wheeling out of dense mists you are filled with expectations of sea and granite and fir vistas and a longing for the sky to clear soon. The birds are blue-gray in flight, but if they catch the morning sun just *so* on their breasts they can flash like freshly minted copper. And when you kill one you can see closely the black tail band and white neck crescent and gaudy, corn-colored beak, and the feet with long, curved black claws for perching, and the pale violet head and breast. After so many years of hunting his delicate cousin the mourning dove, you are always surprised at how large the bandtail is.

I once shouldered my way through a Portland, Oregon, fight crowd so I could shake the hand of Floyd Patterson as he made his way to the dressing room from the ring after giving somebody called Charlie "Emperor" Harris a boxing lesson for six rounds. I reeked of twelve-year-old Jameson, but as I tried to take the former champ's hand I found that mine would not reach around his. In spite of my whiskey courage, that startled the hell out of me. You are startled, and sobered, in much the same way when you pick up the body of a bandtail. The deception comes from the apparent effortlessness of his flight. The flight of a green-winged teal, for instance—a comparable size bird—seems to match his weight as he works as hard as he can to stay aloft: one missed beat, you are certain, and he would plummet. Yet each wing beat of the bandtail surges *him* through the air with the greatest of ease—his wings like sculls sweeping through water—and when he is dead you cannot quite believe that a bird as large as that flew so high and so straight and so fast.

The best way to pursue bandtails is to "get on top of something": few birds will surmount him; he does not seem to relish the company of strangers in his sky. The aesthetics of bandtail hunting demand snow—and if you are a city boy from south of the Mojave and the Tehachapis, snow can be as exotic as unicorns—and plenty of mast crops such as acorns and piñon nuts and salal berries and the Boschian red fruit of the madrone tree. The most obvious advantage of all this feed is that if the birds simply aren't coming in to it, or are so high they resemble a tactical air strike, you can at least forage to your heart's content.

When you reach the top of that "something," you will have done well to have brought along a full-choked shotgun you are sure of and magnum loads, and you should let the bandtails take their time to circle in low enough. They will come in bustling flocks, and you will have to kill them thoroughly. In the parlance, the bandtail is famous for "taking a lot of lead": the way some folks are notorious for holding their Jack Daniel's Old No. 7, the bandtail is notorious for holding No. 6 chilled shot. He will sag when you fire, and there will be a puff of feathers where the shot has hit him; but then he will shake it off the way a fighter shakes a punch and, setting his wings in that unmistakable way which tells you he is dying, he will sail away from any chance you will ever have of finding him, to fall dead beneath a bush three canyons distant and be eaten by a predator more worthy than you. And you will sag a little also as you endeavor to evaluate precisely what brand of low-life son of a bitch you really are for having done such a thing to an animal that supposedly means something to you, that you would probably even go so far as to say you love.

Then another bandtail will spiral in and you will fire and he will drop along that perfect parabola of mortality—so exquisitely sad and beautiful a thing that it transcends all remorse—and because you will be hunting in rough country you will have to scramble to find him lying still and warm in the salal or with his wings spread across a deadfall fir. You will stare at him for a moment before slipping him into your game bag, and for just a moment nothing else in life will be of much importance. There will be a brief intermission from the din of memories of lost girls and fears of where the money is going to come from next and questions of whether you are at all who you think you are that usually fills your head to distraction. You won't pitch your shotgun into the ocean just yet, but promise yourself that if you ever wound another pigeon and cannot find him you will. And hope it never comes to that.

It certainly is a puzzler, all right: you will have killed him because you loved him. Not *destroyed* him because you loved him, only taken his life away. That is the hardest thing, but it is what you will have to grasp if you are going to hunt him, or venture to tell me I may not.

We have entered into a season of the already convinced, and our notions of the wild are as chock-full of feathers as our parkas. We cannot soon forget how the limitless herds of bison and the clouds of passenger pigeons were market-hunted into historical footnotes. Such treasured bits of Americana are freely traded on by those who wish us to accept what passes for Original Sin in these days of Ecology: We don't belong Out There. With our motives for going abroad in the high lonesome suspect at best, we are required to make our way through it like some kind of scrub nurse or lab technician, ironically sterilizing our trespasses with a look-but-don't-touch punctiliousness that entails our carting along all manner of bric-a-brac from the very civilization and technology we contend we are fleeing: our fires spewing from metal canisters, our food (tricked out as some inedible monstrosity called "freeze-dried") rationed out in tidy little foil envelopes better suited to lunar missions than outings, even our speech echoing with the Newspeak of the Technocracy—"biosphere," "ecosystem," "critical habitat." And while all this may even be *necessary* to preserve the little of the real world, the Out There, still remaining, I wonder sometimes if it is entirely in our best interests always to be informed that we are only "visitors" in nature? Do we comprehend the wild any better by reading all the books and all the maps and all the instructions before using? Or, rather, is the wild drifting so far and so irretrievably from our Paleolithic subconsciouses that we would be hard pressed to tell a geoduck from a canvasback without a program, not to mention being able to foretell our fates from the movements of animals or the flights of birds?

So when I tell you I kill bandtails because I love them, yes, you might not quite grasp it. When I reach into the sky with death—

and even if I had never heard of José Ortega y Gasset, there just wouldn't be any other way of putting it—I am not flaunting some supreme arrogance but am practicing something without which this life we lead would seem even more bogus to me than I already feel it to be. Only on the hunting ground—and I have Señor Ortega y Gasset's word on this as well—have I emigrated "from our human world to an authentic 'outside.' " We could argue the right and wrong, even the *logic*, of this till closing time—pounding our fists on the bar, lapsing into angry silences—but if you don't get it, you just don't get it.

Drop by sometime anyway, though. If I have any bandtails stored in the freezer I'll be glad to crack one out for you and broil him up, painting his breast with clarified butter and sprinkling him with salt and paprika. And as you slowly chew his dark flesh, you may begin to taste a wildness that can be recalled only from the dark fringes of memory, and you may come to see what I mean.

You will have to pardon me, however, if in the midst of our meal I should take down my over-and-under and leave you. I will travel until I find a high place to climb up on and walk until everything else is below me. My nostrils will flare like a horse's and be filled with the smell of pines and snow. By the time I stop, my heart will be thundering and the alveoli of my lungs will have expanded to their legendary tennis court of surface area. It will not be dawn yet, but my night vision is good, and I will find a pinecone and pry out some piñon nuts. I will have to remove my gloves to crack them and get at the sweet white kernels. As my fingers numb and my sweat chills and the cold knifes through my beeswaxed boots, I am likely to wonder (possibly in terms somewhat larger than just this mountain or just this morning) what in the *hell* I am doing here all alone, watching this dark sky. Then by shooting light there will be a bandtail on the wing, looking for all the world like a cross between an F-15 and the Paraclete. And as I raise my shotgun, I will know.

Ghost Town, Ghost Bird

The night's final shooting stars shower the far western rim of the Great Basin, trailing yellow fire as they plunge toward this cold desert, flaring out before touching it. A September dawn will soon tint California's eastern side where meltwater rivers flow to no ocean. In a not quite daylight at the end of this dusty washboard road my friend Charley Spiller and I are traveling down, there will be Bodie with its badmen's ghosts and its ghostlike sage grouse. To me that old ghost town always seems more like home than home does.

It is just first light when Charley and I reach the California State Historic Park at Bodie, 8,500 feet up on a hilly plateau of sagebrush. Shooting is prohibited within the boundaries of this once most unbridled gold camp—praised in its day for having the widest streets, the wickedest men, and the "worst climate out of doors"—so Charley and I turn south out of town, following another stretch of dirt road a mile or so to a long sage ridge above a green meadow. The part about the climate, at least, still holds: when we get out of Charley's car this summer's morning we are in bulky down jackets and beginning to shiver in the sharp wind; yet well before noon we will be in shirt sleeves and sweating freely.

We hunt hard for an hour, sweeping the "sage." We are not actually hunting in true sage at all. True sage, the kind that gets sprinkled over sausage meats and poultry stuffings, is an herb of the mint family and a native of the Mediterranean region. For hundreds of years, perhaps longer, folk doctors brewed sage teas as specifics for loss of memory and to increase wisdom. Having no such lofty properties to boast of, silver-gray sage*brush* is merely a North American foliage that smells like sage but is related to the daisy. The only thing sagebrush seems to be good for is providing feed and habitat for sage grouse and other animals. Therefore, I would gladly clear every jar of sage off every spice rack in Italy in exchange for one acre of Great Basin sagebrush.

Hunting in it, however, is still a chore for Charley and me. Neither of us owns a light-footed bird dog, and these giant grouse we're after are invisible unless stepped on. We walk a steady pace—driven as much by the predawn cold as by any hunting instinct—and feel the brush tug constantly at our cuffs.

The sun begins to glimmer off the sawteeth of the high black cordillera of the Sierra Nevada in the western distance, reddening the snow-filled troughs still lingering along the faces of those "Snow-White Craggy Mountains." Charley and I halt now, warmed by our walking, wondering if that far-off sound we hear is the wind or a coyote. Suddenly, standing as still as if they have been waiting there a very long time, wanting to know why we have not recognized their presence sooner, there is a herd of mule deer a hundred yards from us, watching us with their powder-white rumps pointed in our direction. As they turn and amble away, we turn also and see the sun start over the taller line of hills to our east. Their tops must be above 9,000 feet, but from where we stand they are only hills.

As the sunlight flows down the west-facing hillsides, it uncovers old tailings and toppled gallows frames where the earth was gnawed by mine shafts. From where we stand we can also see the sun filling the little pocket in the hills where Bodie lies, like the tide running in under a grounded wreck.

When Bodie lived, it was the hardest town west of Natchez-under-the-Hill. Any genuine "Badman from Bodie"—who in mythical shape was sicced, in lieu of the bogeyman, onto little kids by nineteenth-century mamas—must surely have been someone to contend with: whenever some "curly wolf" out of the surrounding territory wanted to know just how tough he really was, he'd saddle up and ride into Bodie to find out, and was more often than not fitted there with a pine box for his trouble. In its prime between 1878 and 1881, the town was reputed to have had "a man for breakfast" every day as the result of gunfights, stabbings, ambushes, holdups, and simple cussedness. This reputation was well enough founded for one arrival in '79 to report that during his first week in town six fatal shooting matches were carried out—a truce being called for Sabbath observance. A small girl, upon hearing that she and her family were moving from nearby Aurora, Nevada, to the flourishing new mining town, is said to have closed her bedtime prayers by adding, "Good-bye, God; we're going to Bodie!"

Waterman Bodey, a gold-fevered New York Dutchman, is believed to have first found ore on the site of the town that bears his misspelled name in July 1859 while hunting rabbit. Before he could capitalize on his discovery, however, a snowstorm buried him one night a few months later as he struggled unsuccessfully to reach his cabin. For the next fifteen years meager livings were dug out of the ground by the town's small population, until in the mid-1870s rich strikes at the Standard and the Bodie mines began drawing miners from throughout the West's goldfields. By 1881, $25,000,000 in gold and silver had been taken from Bodie Bluff. The town by then could boast four newspapers, three breweries, two banks, a volunteer fire brigade, a Chinatown, hotels, saloons, and some sixty bordellos. The population stood then at roughly fifteen thousand hardy souls variously employed as miners, launderers, bartenders, undertakers, union organizers, claim jumpers, stage robbers, hired gunnies, and prostitutes. Law and order was fitfully maintained by vigilance committees, but to their credit only a single lynching is on record. It must have been a twenty-four-hour Peckinpah movie and a perfectly lovely place in which to reside—as long as you managed to survive mine cave-ins, blizzards, bad whiskey, assorted venereal diseases, and getting shot in the face by hombres with names like "Rough and Tumble Jack."

Then the strikes played out and Bodie's mining stocks crashed in 1883, sending the town into an eclipse from which it never emerged. Until 1932, though, Bodie remained, in the cold, dry air of its high plateau, one of the best-preserved wooden ghost towns the West had to offer. It was in that year, however, that fire razed two-thirds of the business district. Yet much of the town still stands today, and since the early 1960s the state has operated it as a historic park.

Now Charley and I give up on finding any grouse on this south ridge and move back past Bodie and out to a higher ridge running west of town. We leave our jackets in the car and start at the bottom of the ridge and weave our way up through the sagebrush and dust. Here, unlike on the other ridge, we begin to see some grouse sign: clean small heaps of dry elongated pellets of pure sagebrush. We hear sporadic, distant gunfire from other hunters as we climb; but after a difficult hour, which has taken us a little over halfway up the hillside, we stand waist-deep in brush and pant like the retrievers we should own. We agree to swing wide and head down to the car (and there call it quits); but when I turn I see out of the corner of my eye the white flash in the morning sun of grouse's breasts as a covey flares up and lands on top of the ridge above us. I tell Charley and he simply shrugs and without a word we start the hot climb back up again to the grouse habitat.

The sage grouse selects that habitat with some care. First of all it must be within a mile or so of a stream or wet meadow. After finding water, the sage grouse must then find low, sparse sagebrush for his hens to nest in, then thick cover, along the edge of his wet meadow or stream, in which his hens can brood over their chicks in the summer. For winter range—the grouse having flocked together in large numbers in late autumn—he requires south slopes and rocky, windswept ridges where the sagebrush will be kept clear of snow so he can feed. But more than anything else, in the spring the cock must have his traditional strutting ground, or *lek,* in a sagebrush clearing with good visibility. Here he parades and postures and puffs with the other cocks to the delight of the hens— the males occupying specific mating areas of the lek in accordance with hierarchical rankings ranging from the lone master cock to subcocks and guard cocks, all the way out to those forlorn fellows lurking on the edge of the breeding ground like eunuchs outside the harem window.

A master cock may put on his courting performance year after year from within the very same ten-foot-in-diameter "primary mating area" in the lek. And what a performance it happens to be! The ornithologist William Lea Dawson, in his *The Birds of California* ("A Complete, Scientific and Popular Account of the 580 Species and Subspecies of Birds Found in the State"), gives us a vivid description of the "Cock-of-the-Plains" spring dance, first choosing to ascribe its arguably lurid appearance to "Dame Nature's" vengeful efforts to make that "most staid and prosaic of her male progeny appear in a ridiculous light when under the influence of the tender passion." Thus, the male sage grouse

> . . . *first inflates the air-sacs which line his neck until they assume alarming proportions, meeting in front and frequently engulfing his head; the tail with its spiny feathers is spread to the utmost and pointed skyward; then the gallant pitches forward and casts off for a belly-buster slide over the ground, not without much assistance of propulsive feet. . . . As a result of this ridiculous dry-land swim, the feathers of the breast are worn off at the tips till only the quills protrude. These ragged quillends, in being forced over the earth, produce a mild roar which passes for an aria by Caruso with the gray lady in the sagebox. La! but it is absurd! Do you suppose—now do you suppose we ever make such fools of ourselves?*

Even though *I'm* certainly not going to try to answer that, I can say, without fear of contradiction, I believe, that if a master cock can breed forty hens a day (which he is said to be capable of doing), then however absurd his sagebrush hornpipe may look to us, it certainly gets the job done for him.

In the sage grouse's life the role sagebrush plays cannot be overemphasized. While chicks will feed on crickets and grasshoppers for a time, the adult bird's diet is almost exclusively herbivorous, with up to 75 percent of that diet being composed of sagebrush—and in the winter that figure goes closer to 100 percent. The reason for this is that the gizzard of the sage grouse is a soft membranous sac (unlike the strong, muscular, seed-crushing gizzards of more adaptable fowl); and while capable of great distension, it cannot reduce plant material more demanding than the tender shoots of sagebrush, or the forbs in meadows. Yet even on such a seemingly restricted diet the cock sage grouse may reach eight pounds in weight and is second only to the wild turkey in size among our upland game birds.

For the hunter on foot in somewhat open sage country, these second-largest upland game birds will often manage to keep moving all day, out of range, making a long and challenging chase for that hunter. And they are not above taking flight a hundred yards in front of you. It is also my experience that when the sagebrush is heavy, or the birds have just landed from a flight, they may hold tight and get up only when you chance to be within a few feet of them. (I once spent ten minutes circling and circling within six feet of a wounded bird I was searching for, only to have him get up, with a sound like the thudding top rotor of a Sikorsky helicopter, as I was about to step on his tail feathers.) And while they are very hard to see on the ground, when they get up they are not easy to hit and kill, sometimes taking both barrels of magnum-loaded No. 4 chilled shot before going down. For birds as big as they are, they can too readily be missed; but then you have the privilege of seeing them make their long, stiff-winged, cruciform sails far out over the yellow-blooming sagebrush and blue lupine, the chill wind whistling off the tips of their extended primaries.

Where I glimpsed those birds landing was in a jumbled pile of pale stones on the ridgetop. When Charley and I get to within a couple of hundred yards of there, I sucker him into climbing above and around the rock pile and coming down on top of the birds, while I'll go up just a little farther and block the route he will push them down through. Charley agrees, not suckered in the least, knowing he will have a better chance anyway from above of getting the kind of jump shooting he dearly loves.

After about ten minutes of climbing, Charley comes out alone behind the rocks and finds a sage mesa spread before him. Working his way along the edge of it to where I sighted the grouse, he carries his 12-gauge Wingmaster at the ready. Reaching the spot, he sees no birds; but when he takes a few more steps, a single grouse gets up, only four or five feet in front of him. He fires, draws feathers, then pumps and fires again, the bird crumpling and dropping like an origami figure let fall from the hand. Reloading, he starts for the bird, then realizes the unlikelihood of just one bird being here. He moves forward delicately, prepared to walk up more birds; and when he is almost to the dead grouse, four live ones flush right before him. Two more hollow, booming shots, and another bird falls. The rest sail down over the edge of the mesa and past another pile of rocks. I see them coming. They are a little far, but as they drift by like paper kites dropping swiftly, I pull up on the rear one in line and fire twice, watching him flutter and fall after my second shot.

Charley and I meet up again and carry the heavy, warm birds down from the ridge to the car. We lean our empty shotguns against the bumper and clean grouse. (Sage grouse *can* be skinned but will also pluck as easily as a dove—though in either instance they should be drawn quickly to dispel any strong sagebrush flavor.) Charley just happens to have the beneficial fifth of gin lying with the bald spare and oily rags in his trunk, and happily locates a bottle of Rose's lime juice, too, to keep it company. Forgoing all cocktail shakers, we have Kamikazes for breakfast this morning, gargling together alternate sips of lime juice and gin, smearing blood and feathers over the glass of the bottles as we hand them back and forth. We will soon have to find some water to rinse the drawn and featherless birds in. Then we will marinate them in red vermouth overnight and tomorrow part them like chickens on a cutting board, dredge them in flour and brown them in onions and butter, roast them in their marinade and whatever else may come to mind, and then eat their dark, dense, but tender meat as we drink crisp white California wine. For now, though, we drop them into the ice chest, put up the guns, cap the bottles, and mosey into town for one last look.

We park the car in the official lot with its row of flesh-tone fiber-glass outhouses, then walk through town along the weathered boardwalks. Passing the false-fronted buildings with the dusty relics of a different time—all chipped enamel and tarnished brass and cracked wood—seen dimly through the dirty windows, I wonder on which street old "Rough and Tumble Jack" finally met his fate. Charley and I walk on, leaving the town behind as we head for Boot Hill.

In a sagebrush-dotted green meadow we are crossing there appears a large covey of protected sage grouse stepping nervously away from us. I think of what ephemerids these birds must be—like all upland game birds, their population cannot be meaningfully reckoned in terms of a fixed number but rather in terms of upward and downward yearly trends: one or two disastrous hatches and they can flare out like this dawn's shooting stars. Then I realize that where these "valiant sons of the desert" and "grizzled veterans of the wormwood" (as William Lea Dawson stirringly titles them) are stepping is among rusty ore cars and splintered wagon wheels, over the barren foundations of long-gone hurdy-gurdy houses and across the graves of miners who never struck it rich, spreading their spiked tails into the blossom of the desert rose on top of not very ancient human ruins. That's when their ephemerality seems not nearly so profound to me. As we draw up on Boot Hill, the grouse whir low into the thin blue air ahead of us.

Segregated outside Boot Hill's consecrated ground stands a lone tombstone marking the grave of a whore who stayed around too long with the miners who never struck it rich. Inside the cemetery Charley and I wander from chiseled marker to chiseled marker with vague curiosity, considering whose beloved wife lies here, which native of Ireland there, considering all the dead lying where they cannot, short of Judgment Day, whir away either high or low into any blue air. Then I halt in front of one bright white stone and read clearly my own name cut into it and decide that's as deeply as I want to get involved in this particular saga of the West. I tell Charley it's time we made a getaway.

Later we stop along a rocky channel of swift, clear meltwater running through a canyon. Jeffrey pines and piñons cling to the cool walls above us. We rinse the birds, our hands throbbing as we plunge them into the cold river. There is probably some law against rinsing drawn sage grouse in California's trans-Sierra streams. Not that me and Charley give a damn: by this time we're badmen from Bodie anyway.

September Days in the High Sierra

I. Ranch Style

It's not as easy in September, some say. The water is low and the bright elodea weed swishes like the tails of green horses in the fast current. The trout—wild German browns, and all the rainbows a strong temblor spilled out of the upstream hatchery some seasons back—have been fished at doggedly through the spring and summer. Tread too heavily as you stalk from pool to pool, and you will see them streak out from under the cutbank and mass in large schools at the bottom of the main channel. They seem mostly to be on nymphs and other wet feed by September, but at the Ranch the game is to be played with the barbless dry fly exclusively. Name any pattern and it has undoubtedly been thrown at these trout any number of times before during the season. Throw the pattern of your choice and watch them flush like startled wildfowl in the clear cold water of Hot Creek.

Even with all that, I like September there. (Truth to tell, I like May as well, *and* June, July, August, and October—any month, in fact, when I can get onto the east slope of the Sierra Nevada and fish for trout.) By September all the bait fishermen and lead-line trollers are gone from nearby Crowley Lake, and only the tall, elegant masts of sailboats remain on its blue surface. Earlier in the season, when the lake is open to fishing, the call to rent an outboard and load it up with iced beers and warm Velveeta, to put forth and reap a harvest of one- and two-pounders, in short, to bring *in* those sheaves, cannot readily be denied. After Labor Day, however, this particular temptation is removed and it is time to devote oneself to stream fishing. To my way of thinking, this means only one stream, Hot Creek, arguably the finest trout stream in the *entire* Golden State, but certainly the finest the eastern Sierra have to offer.

The most fishable stretch of Hot Creek is not very long—three or four miles—running from below where the creek rises out of a basalt lava table near the hatchery—which supplies millions of trout to Crowley and other eastern Sierra waters, but normally contributes none to self-sustaining Hot Creek—and meanders then across the Ranch property and cuts through the canyon where the public catch-and-release waters are before coming to the public bathing pools where the creek is heated to temperatures beyond the tolerance of trout by natural hot springs and fumaroles.

September finds this public fishing water . . . edgy is the only word for it, and its trout simply callous. Even the weather is out of sorts, with each afternoon producing a thunderstorm of Wagnerian proportion. A fly fisherman making a single-haul cast may note a flash of lightning and count to himself the seconds until the thunder rolls over him; and if it's five seconds or so between light and sound, or as long as he can't smell the ozone or feel his hair stand on end, he'll probably go on casting, never having bothered to lift his eyes from the stream. An earnest fly fisherman can make three thousand casts a day in this manner, come *Götterdämmerung* or high water, and if he lands and puts back a dozen or sixteen trout, he can account himself a wonderful success.

An angler not so earnest, on the other hand, might settle for a couple of rainbows or a single brown for two or three hours' work. One September afternoon, I stood on the bank of the public section of Hot Creek and made hundreds of feeble little roll casts at the same holding brown. I saw him, he saw me, and the point here is that neither of us was much troubled by that: we were both precisely where we wanted to be. Finally, to oblige me, he rose and took my Light Cahill dressed on a No. 14 hook, and I quickly landed him, unhooked him, and fed him back into the creek. Then I walked away from the water and climbed out of the canyon as the afternoon's first bolt of lightning streamed across the gray sky.

The Ranch lies in the meadow above this canyon. It has been catering to dry-fly fishermen since the early 1940s. Its biggest all-time brown weighed 14¾ pounds. The Ranch employs a fish culturalist who cares for the creek, dredging and preening it, seeing to its aquatic insect yield and manicuring its spawning beds, like a Buddhist tending a Zen garden. Yet by September the Ranch's looked-after fish are just as callous as the ones in the canyon below, maybe more so. In the face of such trout obstinacy, the Ranch's strict allegiance to the dry fly has been called "hard core" by many anglers. Exactly so.

Early in the morning, passing up breakfast in order to steal a march on the day, I take out from my cabin with my eight-foot No. 6 graphite rod. I cross the sprinklered green lawn in front of the cabins, then the wooden footbridge over the creek, and enter the meadow, its unsprinklered sere grass sawing at my boot tops. I go a mile or so downstream, staying wide of the water, until I have to recross the creek on another bridge. Here there is a brass plaque hammered into the lava rock above the bridge, honoring a dead rod maker and master angler of perhaps no more than local renown. I read the sentimental words and wish I'd had a chance to fish with him.

Once over the bridge, I swing back out away from the bank to avoid notifying the trout of my arrival and to keep out of a large boggy area. As I walk, I catalog my equipment in my head. Vest and hat and polarized glasses, flies and fly dressing and tippet material, clippers and license and stainless-steel hemostats. I am set, I would say.

It is still cold, even in the sun, and steam rises off the water in wispy billows. I am thinking I must have the entire creek to myself *this* early. I plan on going all the way to the fence line marking the end of the property, then fishing my way back with surgical skill. But when I come around the last rock outcropping on the trail, I see another angler already out ahead of me on the final stretch of water.

I watch him cast. I wonder if he was here in time to see the sunrise, or maybe he just stood by the stream all night, a weary sentinel fingering his tackle. Well, I think, this part's his now; he's earned it. I trek back a good distance above him and start in.

In this portion of the creek the water is quite shallow in places, riffling over the smoothly worn gravel. As I begin to work it, I cannot seem to interest any of the trout I see in the fly I am throwing. It's a Ginger Quill; the night before, as I looked over the hand-tied flies for sale in the Ranch office—plastic boxes with scores of compartments, each filled with multicolored imitations, the nearest approximation to a candy counter in the life of a fly fisherman—another angler indicated this No. 16 and told me, "Good Lord, man, get something with some *brown* in it!" So I did, and now as the trout move steadily upstream away from me and my fly with the brown in it, all I can do is follow.

The river bends around a sheer cliff, the morning sun on the rock face turning it the color of buckskin. There is a large deep pool here under the cliff, and when I work my way up to it, I find it filled with rising trout!

Yesterday, when I had been out on the creek in the afternoon, I hadn't seen one fish break the surface. Then, very late in the day, I had concluded it was the most propitious moment for changing flies, an act inspired in equal measure by primitive superstition and by sheer boredom. And as I tried to tie on my latest choice in an artificial, my newest offering to the Great God Trout, there appeared before me a hatch and with it rainbows in great multitude boiling out of the creek.

I have never had so much difficulty with a knot as I had with that one then. It took me five minutes to assemble an improved clinch, what with my looking up at the water every few seconds and whimpering. At last I had it tied. I gathered up my loose line and lurched toward the creek, only to discover it smooth as a sheet of vinyl, the hatch over and the trout settled back to the bottom.

Now, this morning, there are before me in this pool dozens of dun-feeding browns and rainbows, including one for-sure two-pounder, and I have no intention of changing flies. I am utterly giddy as I launch my first cast and watch it land in a tangle of floating line right in the middle of all those fish. When they show little alarm at the wad of pink six-weight passing over them, however, I know this was meant to be my day.

My casting after that does not, as you might imagine, become suddenly sober and expert; it becomes crazed. It is *cast, cast, cast, cast, cast, cast, cast, strike, miss, cast, cast, cast.* . . . Then a rainbow comes up, lifting his head out of the water far enough for me to see the deep redness of his gill cover and the dull platinum sheen of his mouth as it opens and he takes my fly. I raise my rod tip and he is on. He dances—a buck-and-wing it looks like—across the pool and the green weed banks until I bring him to shore. I pick him up for a second in order to remove the fly from his lip, then, kneeling, slip him back into the fast, chill water, none of the other trout seeming to be even slightly aware yet of what's taking place.

I fish this pool all morning. I have on some two dozen trout and manage to land ten of them, including a very nice and very feisty wild brown. I hold him up a moment—careful though not to squeeze the life out of him with the old "Montana handshake" as they call too ardent a grip up Yellowstone way—and marvel at the compact brutishness of this little spotted fin-monster. Returning him to the current, I start casting again.

All morning it has been that two-pounder I have truly been trying for, but he has disdained my every offer. I keep on tossing the Ginger Quill at him, until, looking down at my vest, I see a large gray mayfly spinner clinging to it. I pick the insect off and hold her up to the light and see her glow. Turning her loose, I think, in spite of my misfortune the day before, it is time to change flies. I put on a California Mosquito and lay it out in front of the big 'bow, and on about the fifth toss I get it right and he takes. He goes through the pool in what can only be described as a sequence of violent upheavals, and I hang on like a saddle-bronc rider praying for the eight-second whistle. A good two or three seconds shy of even that mark, however, he cleans me off, breaking the hook in two and slashing away downstream.

Trembling, I tie on a new fly. The last contest, however, has finally alerted all the trout, and the pool just isn't the same after that. I have now stood at this creekside so long that to my eye the moving water has become the sole *unmovable* object in the known universe, everything else having been set in motion to glide past me. Before I know it, it has gotten to be midafternoon and my belly is growling. I have to shake my head to clear it of the afterimages of tailing trout that appear behind my eyelids every time I blink. I reel up and start the long walk back to my cabin. Crossing the footbridge by the memorial plaque, I spot what looks like a pair of genuinely tremendous trout whirling and thrashing in the current in some kind of dogfight. An old man chases along the bank after them, throwing his fly out again and again and shouting to his wife downstream, "They're coming! They're coming!" I head on.

Sunset finds me on the porch of my cabin, tasting the high country in a drink of tequila and grapefruit juice, listening to the distant song of a coyote pack. I sit there until nightfall, watching the mountains grow dark, the nighthawks dip in the air, the fish culturalist in his wet suit toil with a pitchfork in the September creek.

II. Ah, Wilderness!

In September the morning air at 9,000 feet has the rawness of late fall to it, and the horse's brown tail makes a raspy sound as it swishes across his croup. I have on my down jacket and feel under my right leg the aluminum rod case tied along the saddle. The trail I ride is of decomposed granite and comes out of a shady grove of lodgepole pine to skirt the edge of Tunnel Meadow. There are any number of meadows to choose from here in the Golden Trout

Wilderness of the eastern Sierra, all having likely golden-trout water running through them. Some are called Ramshaw, others Templeton or Mulkey or Little Whitney. Where the trail forks I take the upper route, the trail that will carry me to the meadow called Big Whitney.

At the top of a long switchback I pause to let my horse blow, then start him down the grade on the other side. The ground is white from the granite sand, and around me are dead ponderosas gnarled and scarred by lightning strikes: the penalty for reaching too high. The big chestnut gelding I am astride walks briskly and swings away from low-hanging branches without my having to rein him around in the slightest: by the time the trail leads us down into the willows lining Golden Trout Creek, I think I must be in love with this noble creature. Then above us some jet jockey punches past Mach 1, and as he streaks away from the wave of his sonic boom, drawing a vapor trail as fluffy as cotton across the sky behind him, I am left below to try to stay with what has just become for me a half-ton of bounding dog food.

The wilderness rapidly passing by me at this moment is the country of the California golden trout, the little trout with the grand Latin name of *Salmo aquabonita,* the trout of beautiful water. Ten thousand or so years ago, these fish were most probably typical rainbows, but through lava flows and other geological change they became isolated in these high-mountain headwaters of the Kern River and evolved into the golden of today. They are now also found elsewhere because of transplantation (one Colonel Sherman Stevens is said to have taken a dozen of the tiny goldens out of Mulkey Creek in 1876 and packed them over the Great Basin–Pacific Divide in a teapot, pouring them at journey's end into fishless Cottonwood Creek near his sawmill. It is believed it was descendants of these same fish that the biologist David Starr Jordan used in 1892 as specimens for the first scientific description of the species). Although resident elsewhere now, as I said, the goldens' source remains two creeks, Golden Trout Creek and the South Fork Kern, and their tributaries.

The South Fork Kern runs down the middle of Tunnel Meadow, and Golden Trout Creek passes just beyond its western end, the two water systems almost joining at that point. During the last century, someone actually attempted (who *knows* why?) to dig a tunnel there and do to the two creeks what the aeons had not. He failed, but left the meadow with a name. The goldens of the two creeks are considered subspecies of each other: one darker, one lighter; one with fewer spots, one with more. I'll take either kind, counting them among nature's lucky breaks. Like getting money from home without having to write for it.

The chestnut gelding ceases to bound now, and we continue on in a more orderly fashion. The creek canyon here is narrow and cool. I see a light reddish, summer-coated doe with two fawns, a big redtail hawk in a dead pine, and later, the dusty Herefords that are permitted to graze these high meadows. Seven miles on the trail from Tunnel Meadow the canyon widens and opens onto the large natural pasturage of Big Whitney Meadow. The altitude I have ridden to is now over 9,600 feet and the air is as thin as a whispered promise. I ride the horse up into the timber fringing the meadow and dismount. I tie him up short to a young tree and out of the saddlebags come lunch, my fishing vest, and a cool beer. Untying the leather thongs holding my rod case to the saddle, I carry the case over to a rock and sit down to rig up my eight-foot graphite rod and eat my San Francisco salami and Tillamook cheese sandwich. Finishing my beer, I put on my polarized glasses and head out of the trees and down to Golden Trout Creek.

The sun at such a height can cut into your hide like a branding iron, but the open water sparkling under it this afternoon is without a doubt *aquabonita*. Would I care to call this water "gin clear"? Like hell! How *anyone* could ever compare the look of a swift, cold trout creek to that vile swill of tosspots—and the occasional sage-grouse hunter—has always been beyond me. No, at the right time, in the right light, Golden Trout Creek assumes the appearance, not of some foul intoxicant, but of a vein of pure diamond skilled lapidaries have painstakingly gone over with polishing wheels and jewelers' rouge.

I come to the creek's brush-free edge and proceed upstream after its trout. This often means crawling on my belly like a snake through the warm grass, or at the very least finding a large rock to conceal myself behind while I cast. The goldens are flighty enough to demand such stealth, yet compensate for this by being quick to take any and all flies that float their way. I flip No. 18 Sierra Bright Dots and No. 20 Royal Wulffs—dry flies of microscopic dimensions—onto the goldens, and they accept either with the surging eagerness of newborn pigs locating the tit. They fight, too, running full out until the 6X tippet turns them, putting an actual bend in the rod, then lashing vigorously in the air as they are lifted into it, showing more strength and courage, gram for gram, than trout five and ten times their size. *Of course* they're small—six to eight inches in length and only a scant few ounces in weight—but if you could somehow find in these high, nutrient-poor Sierra creeks a fighting golden the size of a steelhead, then you would have to have, bar none, the world's champion trout on your hands. And then there is their color.

Nothing quite properly prepares you for the look of the first California golden trout you take from a creek and hold in your hand. His tail and dorsal fin are spotted, his back and parr marks the color of Spanish olives, his belly running anywhere from banana to cadmium to gold, the stroke of color along his lateral line like grenadine mixed with orange juice. What he most looks like as he flutters in your hand is either a terrible drink or a goddamn Technicolor sunset! The golden trout, alone among the animals of the chase, is an object of *virtu* Fabergé would have concealed unadorned inside one of the Easter eggs he fashioned for the tsars.

I catch and uncatch thirty or forty of these twenty-four-karat fish between noon and three o'clock this day on Golden Trout Creek. Four others I kill and clean, the biggest one a full eight inches long. I leave the creek and return to my horse in the trees. I place the fish and my vest back into the saddlebags and retie my rod case along the saddle. Mounting up, I start on in.

Tonight, in camp, I will place thin slices of onion and lemon inside these fish and bake them in tinfoil. They will be delicate and delicious, and even now will still be among the most beautiful of fish. Tomorrow I will try the South Fork Kern in Tunnel Meadow, taking it one pool at a time, casting from behind its tall willows to individual fish, seeing if I can detect the subtle differences between

South Fork goldens and Golden Trout goldens, only to realize at day's end how little profit is to be found in that sort of analysis: a golden is a golden is a golden, thank heaven.

At the end of *this* Sierra day, however, there is one final sight to see. When the horse carries me back over the ridge and down into Tunnel Meadow, the distant hills across from me are already like folds of velvet material as the shadows begin to move up them. Then in the meadow I see a lone coyote sitting placidly, staring at those hills, his coat gray and long and fixed for winter. I suddenly feel wild as a coyote myself in this golden country, and I stand up in the stirrups and yip out loud at the little prairie wolf. His head turns toward me, but he does not know what to make of this misshapen horse-thing. I yip again, and the chestnut gelding beneath me grows skittish. The coyote stands and gives me one last look before swinging off in a stiff-legged coyote lope. I wave *adiós* to him and give the horse a kick to send us galloping on into camp.

As I gallop, the cool evening air rushing by me, I think: Nope, a wilderness doesn't always have to be a realm of epic struggles or giant beasts. Sometimes just the little things, like a coyote in a meadow at sunset or a golden trout rising to a fly, will do.

And yes, I have to admit, those golden trout sure are small. But then I ask, How big exactly *does* a nugget of true gold have to get before it is of true value?

The Geography of Dove

I was sitting here, trying to remember all the places dove have led me in this life. It doesn't seem possible that a couple of ounces of bird would be capable of leading anyone anywhere; but it's either that or they have been tailing me all this time. I'm inclined to believe that it must be the former.

Where they first led me, at the age of eleven, was across a barbed-wire fence and into a pasture of turkey millet where I stood with my 20-gauge hugged against my chest, watching the sun burn its way above the Sierra's jagged crest. I could smell the San Joaquin Valley soil warming beneath my sneakered feet; then I saw a mourning dove in flight. For the first time in my life I swung a gun at a bird on the wing and fired. And saw a bird die. I walked to him and picked up the first game animal I had ever killed. Yes, I whooped some, but there was another thing, too, some other feeling, that I have been trying for the last two decades to put my finger on, that made that dove, which I eventually made myself slip away in my too-long game bag, seem to weigh in my hand far in excess of what one could ever have suspected.

For two decades now I have returned to that part of the Valley each season, even though the changing face of agriculture there has left the hunting not what it once was, to hunt dove. And those dove hunts, with their enduring rituals of the noisy restaurant dinner the night before opening day; the cool hum of the air conditioner in the dark motel room when I am too excited to sleep; the predawn shuffling out to the car and the sight down the row of motel rooms of all the other dove hunters—strangers to us, yet all of us brought to this Valley by the same little bird—shuffling out; the fast drive on the straight, unlighted country road out to our friends the Dutros' ranch, where we drink coffee before heading out to the field or pasture or dry sinking basin, wherever Elmer Dutro has seen dove in August's last days; then our morning shoot—some years my shotgunning skills worthy of praise, others pitifully poor, or at any rate that's the way the dove made them seem—then back to Elmer's to pluck and clean the birds in the shade of a tall cottonwood in his yard, the men having that first, always-best cold beer of the hot day, the children curious as to its taste, the dogs waiting patiently for somebody to lob them a delicacy sorted out of the dove's entrails, before Mary Dutro calls us in for one of her farm breakfasts of eggs and pancakes and Portuguese sausages, and *more* eggs and pancakes and Portuguese sausages; then the afternoon siesta; the afternoon shoot in the blistering heat; more dove to clean; and in the warm evening, in the Dutros' cool adobe house, one of the world's truly grand farm dinners of blood-rare roast beef, garden tomatoes and red onions sliced up together in a vinaigrette sauce, roasted buttered potatoes, cold milk, pie, and vanilla ice cream—in this day when a diet of leafy greens and sprouted grains, with just a smidgen of yogurt on the side, is believed to hold the secret to eternal life, one wonders if the honest-to-God farm meal must not be fast becoming an endangered species. If so, one also wonders why so many of the egg-meat-and-potato-eating farmers one has known have all managed to *live* so damn long—those dove hunts became for me a fixed point in the changeable course of a year, a landmark to head for. Coming at the start of the hunting season, they were my New Year's Day.

There have been other places, as well, that dove have led me to. On the Njugini River in southern Kenya, I found them. I was shooting sandgrouse (a grouse-shaped pigeon, high fast-flyers coming in to the water from over the yellow thorn trees), birds quite foreign to me. I never really know what to think when I first kill an animal that is foreign to me; there is something so *impersonal* about it. But the sandgrouse were certainly coming in most energetically, and hunting strangers—especially plump, gray, darting, swift strangers—is much preferable to hunting nothing at all. Then some dove appeared in the morning light—don't ask me which one of the several hundred varieties; they were just unquestionably dove—and after I'd taken a few of them, things were all right again and I wasn't feeling so much like some geeky *tourist* anymore. It was like rounding an unfamiliar corner to find my home waiting for me there.

In another September I found myself getting off a jet airliner in Memphis, Tennessee, following dove, and hearing my good friend the eminent bear hunter Fred Fortier of Ripley, Mississippi, who had come to fetch me, announce, "Well, Tom, I had my choice of three dove hunts we could go to, so I settled on the one with the best party!" And while down in the Delta country of Mississippi the dove hunting itself proved only fair to middling that year, and the weather turned out to be some of the hottest I had ever experienced, the party afterward at the shotgun house down by the Sunflower River, where the dove were barbecued to a tee, a mighty fine rock 'n' roll band played long into the night, such luminaries as Doug Mauldin, Louie Devereux, and Blinky Evans were in attendance, along with lovely and gracious Southern ladies too numerous to mention, and the whiskey flowed convivially, was indeed one of the best parties in my memory, though something of a disappointment to those who had been present at the previous year's festivities— those having been capped by a rousing good fistfight involving a fair percentage of the male attenders and lasting for what seemed hours. Oooh, but you should have been here *last* year, son, more than one partygoer informed me, tapping his jangling bourbon glass against my sweaty shirt front. One must never underestimate the positive effect a good party will have on one's opinion of a dove hunt.

The promise of exceptional dove hunting even led me once to Cuba, to Ciego de Ávila Province in the island's central green farmlands, where the mourning dove is considered, as most dove are in Latin America, a major agricultural pest. There the limit was so generous and the birds flying so strongly, that after two hours of shooting over a cut rice field, and still well shy of my limit, I just shook my head and told my bird boy, *"No más, no más,"* and much to his delight handed him my 12-gauge and the remainder of my Italian-manufactured shells and let him shoot some birds for himself. Anytime hunting or fishing gets *so* good that downing another bird or landing another fish becomes no more than a mechanical reaction, with the feelings and emotions, if not cut off, then at least seriously numbed, it is time to quit for the day, to step on back and appraise the situation. No sense in going for a record: somebody else will always achieve a higher body count. There were more than enough dove taken that day, anyhow, to give the bird boys full game bags to carry home and to give us a monumental dove dinner at the state-run hotel that night, where my friend Steve Stathatos and I bypassed everything else on the menu and ate more dove at one sitting than anyone ever dreamed two people could eat.

Leading, then, even as I was taking my lead on him, *is* what the dove must have been doing to me all these years. And as he leads me into my twentieth season as a hunter, I realize that there is more to it than merely the states and countries he has taken me to. Another sort of geography has been involved. Because as I look back on it now, I see that where that small grayish bird has taken me, ultimately, is from childhood into adulthood. And with the possible exception of the one running from here to the end, life has no longer road.

Turkey Wild: First Impressions

I saw them for the first time on the road outside Raton, New Mexico, after a hard, cold elk hunt. They always seem to be trying to make a fool out of me by taking on different shapes, and this first time they appeared as a herd of mule deer feeding in a stubble field at the edge of a timber stand.

"Look at all those damn deer," I said to my friend Tom Davis, wistfully shaking a head filled with carnivorous lusts.

"Those aren't deer!" Tom just about screamed as we both craned around to get a better look. He was right.

The next time I saw them I was in another speeding vehicle, this one crossing the hill country of Texas, my dozing head lolling against the passenger window. Prying my eyelids open, I squinted into the early morning sun, then around at the hardscrabble terrain.

Now they were just off the highway, strutting machines made out of bright mica. I sat up so fast I nearly rammed my poor skull through the roof. They were gone.

The third time was on the big island of Hawaii as I hunted wild goats and sheep and pigs. I had left behind the blood-colored volcanic ground full of lava tubes and war trails and ancient ghosts in feathered capes, and was walking in rolling green country not unlike that of the California coast range in springtime. I had seen many of the island's simple-minded nene geese waddling around pacifically, and when I topped a small grassy rise and a flock of birds detonated in front of me, I thought for just a moment that that's what they were. But as I saw those huge fowl sailing heart-stoppingly away, I knew I'd been fooled again, fooled by wild turkeys.

In spite of such sightings, I think it came to me pretty much as a surprise, when it finally did come to me, that I wanted to hunt wild turkeys something fierce. The main problem was that the wild turkey does not occur naturally in my state of California. Of course, back in the Late Pleistocene there was, according to A. W. Schorger, author of *The Wild Turkey: Its History and Domestication*, the now extinct species of turkey or near-turkey known as *Parapavo californicus*, and from the black goo of the La Brea tar pits on Wilshire Boulevard in L.A. they do keep pulling out bits and pieces of him—along with bits and pieces of camels, mastodons, pygmy antelope, and the stray hunter-gatherer—but that seemed to be it as far as wild turkeys were concerned. Nobody I knew had ever hunted wild turkeys in California, and so I began thinking in terms of expeditions mounted to such far-off wild turkey havens as Florida, Mississippi, or Alabama.

Then I began to hear, almost as a whisper, that for some years my very own California Department of Fish and Game had been wild-trapping Rio Grande turkeys in Texas and turning them loose out here just for me, it would seem. On further investigation I found that in fact there were now over 30,000-and-counting of the birds gobbling from one end of the state to the other, with, to boot, open seasons on either sex in the fall and on gobblers only in the spring. This news was almost too portentous to contemplate—I

could actually hunt wild turkeys without ever leaving California!—
so I responded to it in the only sensible way I could: I went berserk.

In that condition, I firmly believed that the most important
thing in the world was learning how to sound just like a wild
turkey. Toward this end I wrote the noted wild-turkey expert Dave
Harbour, explaining my state of mind to him. He seemed to
understand my ravings and to sympathize, and quickly sent me two
diaphragm mouth calls, one a Super Double "D" with twin latex
reeds, the other a 3-D Omega with triple reeds, to be taken as
needed. I trimmed those two calls up right away, fitted them
against the roof of my mouth, and proceeded to produce noises
faintly like those made by a whoopee cushion.

Dave had also urged me to seek professional help in the form of
a recording demonstrating the various calls one can make to attract
wild turkeys. After a few days of making little more than plaintive
blats on my new mouth calls, I relented and purchased a tape by a
champion of the calling art and jammed it into the cassette deck in
my auto. Thinking I was in business now that I had this teaching
aid, I would sail, on the soaring concrete of the freeway system, over
the urban sprawl of Greater Los Angeles, the power windows sealed,
the air conditioner adjusted to "Permafrost" in March, tonguing a
rubber mouth call against my palate and trying to perfect the "call
of the lost hen," "lost gobbler yelps," "assembly calls," and the
Chinese algebra of the "kee-kee run." When the cassette machine
finally ate the tape—no doubt in an effort to *tell* me something—I
did not hesitate one second in going out to buy a record.

Visiting friends, I would be offered a glass of chilled white
wine to sip while they'd gently turn up the latest release of such
avant-gardists as Captain Beefheart or Philip Glass on their state-of-
the-art sound systems. Friends unwise enough to visit me, on the
other hand, would be pressed to have a hit from the jug and
subjected to "Mr. Turkey Himself" or "Sweet Sounding Yelper"
throbbing out of my hardly grandiose record player. There was some
danger of my becoming a pest.

Yet even after going to such lengths, I was still showing no
discernible proficiency as a caller of wild turkeys. However, on
taking up an autographed copy of Dave Harbour's *Hunting the*

American Wild Turkey (a courtly tribute to *Meleagris gallopavo*—
Dave's game bird of choice for "many long and joyous years"), I soon
found that it was a far less complex matter, this turkey calling, than
I was trying to turn it into. Let me quote Dave's eminently sensible
words on the subject:

> *First, and foremost, the spring gobbler hunter should concentrate on learning
> only two simple calls: the cluck and the low yelp of the hen. Being able to
> reproduce these two calls reasonably well can get the new hunter almost as
> many turkeys as an expert who can make twenty different calls with perfection.*

Such words, perhaps a *bit* vague grammatically but still
heartfelt, were to me like fresh air after being cooped up in a class on
phenomenalist philosophy. I immediately narrowed the scope of my
studies, and as the spring gobbler season neared I was producing a
passable yelp. It sounded so good to me, in fact, that I almost felt
bad when, realizing I didn't have the faintest idea where to start
looking for any of the state's 30,000-plus wild turkeys, I went out
and hired a guide to show some of them to me.

I made the long drive up through the San Joaquin Valley and
into the Sacramento in an Easter Sunday shower, passing farmhands
in the grain fields along the freeway—the heads of the new barley
brushing their waists, making them look like waders in a green surf
as they set out irrigation pipes in the rain. Tehama County at the
north end of the northern valley is well regarded for its population
of Rio Grande turkeys, and late in the afternoon I exited the cement
river of Interstate 5 at Red Bluff and wound my way out an oak-
lined country road to meet my guide Mike Ballew, manager of Dye
Creek Preserve, which was offering its first season of guided turkey
hunts.

The next morning at four o'clock, the moon—one day past
full—still high in the now cloudless night sky, we loaded our gear
into Mike's Bronco and set off for his turkey hunting ground near
Jelly's Ferry on the wide Sacramento River. The hunting ground
was a large hilly piece of property behind a gate with a padlock on
it. Opening the gate and following a dirt road by moonlight, we

could make out long wild grass, oaks and Digger pines, white-faced cattle still bedded down, and a realtor's sign offering parcels for subdivision. Parking the Bronco, we started off for higher ground on foot through the darkness which, after that sign, seemed much chiller to me.

After ten minutes of fast travel, the darkness now graying toward dawn, we walked out onto a listening point, and for the first time in my life I heard the clear, full gobble of a wild turkey. Mike nodded, and we hurried down into the draw below, closing the gap between us and the tom.

We came to a fallen oak in a large clearing and set ourselves up. Burrowing down behind the oak, I was dressed in camouflage pants, camouflage shirt, camouflage hat, camouflage mask, camouflage gloves—even my 30-inch-barrel Wingmaster Mag was *painted* in camouflage. Then Mike took out his well-used wooden Lynch box call, chalked it up, and yelped. The gobbler answered at once, sounding almost on top of us—though probably still over 150 yards out. But there we were, talking to a different species, speaking an alien tongue. We conversed in that tongue for three hours that morning, hearing besides our first tom half a dozen other gobblers and fifty or sixy distinct gobbles.

Against our better judgment, and that of about every known turkey expert, we tried to move up on that first gobbler when, after an hour of calling, he still refused to come in and our patience had given out. We crossed back over the snaking draw (on the chance that that obstacle was what was keeping him from coming to us) and climbed the side of a steep hill—Mike wondering under his breath why the hills always seemed to get steeper every year, and deciding it must be erosion. The two of us, wandering among the trees with our faces behind net masks, resembled figures risen from some surrealist's canvas. We found a new blind at the base of a California oak and set up shop again for Mike to yelp and cluck and gobble.

There could be hardly a lovelier time or place to sit waiting to kill a gobbler than in the morning in the hills of the northern Sacramento Valley in early spring. That is when the new grasses smell most peppery, the limbs of the manzanitas have acquired the hue of certain young beaujolais, geese are honking overhead near the sun, and hoppers begin to tick softly all around. You can sit on the gnarled root of an old oak and turn these charming thoughts over in your head until you have to shift your butt off that gnarled old root, and in shifting thus you may catch a glimpse of something up the hill from you. And turning your head, you might *just* be able to see pearly primaries at the ends of big dark wings beating through the luminous air and heading rapidly off.

When Mike and I walked up to the spot to see what had gone wrong, we found the gobbler's trail through the dewy grass where, without a sound, he had come down to stand right behind us and stare—until I moved. We followed the trail back to an ancient Digger pine roost tree where we found the long J-shaped droppings of gobblers and the round popcorn ones of hens—all fresh. We walked on over the country—now silent of gobbles at midmorning—Mike showing me where the turkeys had turned over platters of cow manure to get at the worms and grubs underneath. Toward noon—closing time during the spring season—he spotted a tom with two hens on a hill two draws distant. To me the tom looked big and black as a nervous wild boar as Mike sat there calling to him, calling, "Come to me, come to me," all to no avail.

The next morning, thin clouds over the waning moon, Roy Fears, vice-president of the California State Chapter of the National Wild Turkey Federation, and I are scurrying out along a ridge on the same Jelly's Ferry property—a pig hunter having come in this morning and Mike Ballew having had to guide him. Roy Fears wears a sweated-through Stetson, a turkey feather in the band and a button declaring him an "All-American Turkey" pinned to the back of the crown; and he has a gobbler talking to us ardently. Roy halts abruptly, peers out the ridge in the dim morning light, then wheels on me. His eyes unquestionably go *boing.*

"Get down" he hisses desperately, pulling his net mask over his hat and face. I put on my own mask and belly into the grass at the base of an oak snag, barely avoiding a steaming pile of Hereford droppings. Mosquitoes crash into my back, buttocks, and thighs like flaming Zeroes into the deck of a carrier. Roy calls once more, perfectly, and one instant later I see three bearded gobblers running down the ridge toward us.

As the turkeys run, their bodies rock from side to side like empty boxcars on a downgrade. The biggest one, still in full trot, fans his tail and drops his wings, and my heart goes pitter-pat. The turkeys pass right in front of us and I have an open running shot at the biggest. But I can't be certain, so I wait, hoping Roy can call them in closer. Then the birds get behind a brush pile, and all I can see is their bobbing, flicking jittery heads. The biggest one's is blue as Indian jewelry. I keep waiting for that sure killing shot; and until it comes, I will not risk crippling one of these fowl.

After a few minutes of toying with us, however, the turkeys grow bored—that's the way I like to look at it, anyway—and with a *purrt, purrt, PURRT* they are into the air exactly like some kind of the most God-awful-big quail anyone has yet imagined, flying aloft, as the Missourian Mark Twain once described it, "with the rush and whir of a shell." And there I am on the ground, slipping the safety back on my 12-gauge, a fool again.

I did learn one or two things, though, from my first time out after wild turkey in my native state. I learned, for instance, that you can practice calling with a record, and pick up calling tips from authorities, but it is the wild turkey himself, ultimately, who teaches you how really to call. I also learned that the wild turkey and turkey hunting have a rather sunny future in sunny California. And I learned that not only would I be back after wild turkeys next season, but I was still about as berserk as when I started out.

Because less than a week later I am on Santa Catalina Island in the Pacific off Los Angeles, pursuing Spanish goats and wild pigs with my four-wheel compound bow and my friends George Papac and Steve Stathatos. There are transplanted Rio Grande turkeys on the island, I have heard, and in the foggy wet dawn on one of the island's green ridges I am tempted to try and have a word with them, even though I cannot hunt them. When I hear a gobble in the dense toyons below me, though, I am no longer tempted—I am compelled.

I set my bow aside and slip the blue diaphragm against the roof of my mouth. Steve and George laughed when I sat down to play before, annoyed at my interminable practicing. Now I cup my hands around my mouth and make my first tentative calls to a wild turkey. In a flash he answers, and nobody's laughing anymore. We're all beaming like lunatics as this voice from the Out There comes to us and we begin, of all impossible things, to converse.

A Day at the Bear Races

How to hunt black bear? Let me count the ways.

One way, of course, is spotting-stalking, the same method by which most everything else gets hunted. And it does account for a lot of the black bear taken every year, though with such an evasive and wary creature it is by no means the surest way. Another way, where legal, is to set yourself up over something dead and rank-smelling and wait for a bear to shamble by underneath. All *this* requires is much patience and a strong stomach. The way I like best, however, in the dense-coniferous-forest canyons of northeastern California, is the way of hound, racing after a pack of them with a black bear leading us on.

One day in November I stood on a logging road in this part of

California, in Shasta County, north of the town of Redding, and listened to a bear guide's pack of Walker hounds barking "wall-to-wall" below us in a dense-coniferous-forest canyon. And felt my heart leap against the cage of my ribs. The guide was listening too, and he could tell by the sound of his hounds' voices that the race was done. Down there, a black bear was already up a tall fir tree. He got his packboard, I got my rifle, and we headed down.

Hounds and houndmen are not like you and me. A hound is not made for bringing you the Sunday paper, honoring a point, or retrieving a gadwall. He is made for trailing and running larger mammals, treeing them, or baying them on the ground and catching them, to hold for a hunter. Houndmen, if they are true houndmen, would rather run their dogs in the woods than spend an all-expense-paid week in Paris, France. They'd rather listen to their dogs give voice than Hank Williams sing "Jambalaya." I have heard that the first thing some of the superannuated-hippie ranchers of California's marijuana belt think of to do with their not insubstantial harvest money is (forget the Mercedes!) to plonk a big chunk of it down on a fully trained pack of bear hounds and a 4 × 4 pickup with dog boxes. It is hard to know if houndmen were made for hounds or vice versa, but they were certainly made for each other.

It was cold in the shadows of this canyon as we skidded and slid through the loose soil on the steep slope. As we slashed obliquely down toward the rocky stream bed running along the bottom we could hear the Walkers barking with each of their breaths, the way they do when they have an animal treed. Then we'd drop into one of the feeder creeks running into the larger stream, and the wall of the creek bed and the noise of the running water would cover the sound of the dogs. But when we climbed back out, there they would be again, giving voice still.

Houndmen of various regions have their own consensuses about which breeds of hound they prefer to hunt behind. In Shasta County, for instance, Walkers seem to be the breed of choice. If a houndman from another neck of the woods, where they hunt bear with another kind of dog, were to move to Shasta County with his pack, he would find himself in time, as his hounds aged, drawing from the available gene pool and replacing them with Walkers.

Houndmen look for a variety of qualities in their dogs. Some want a dog with a good nose; others, stamina. Many want flat-out speed. "Everybody breeds for fastness," the guide told me one afternoon as we were rolling down the road out of the mountains toward Redding in his old green pickup. "I don't breed for fastness. I breed for heart and ability." He paused and stared out at the two-lane blacktop getting sucked up under the hood. "But mostly heart," he added, nodding his head.

Around the age of five a hound is in his prime, physically and mentally, and is probably worth in excess of a thousand dollars if he has been trained by an expert houndman. By age seven he has begun to top out and is no longer leading the pack. But if he has "heart and ability," his days as a bear dog are far from numbered. An older, more experienced, *wiser* animal is invaluable as a strike dog to scent out a trail when the ground is cold or the track old or tangled. This is something the years teach a hound's nose, and it can keep him running game until he can't run anything anymore.

At last we had worked our way down along the face of the slope to where we could see the hounds surrounding the base of a tree, the dogs standing on their hind legs, leaning with their front paws up on the bark of the tree, yelping wildly. You might not think that traveling downhill ought to be much of a chore, but after hurrying headlong into a deep canyon, following the sound of dogs, my chest was heaving, sweat poured off me, and my calf muscles were trembling in pain. Then I saw, thirty feet up the tree, the chocolate-brown bear perched on the lowest limb, staring quizzically at all these barking beasts below him—seeming to him to be like so many snapping and roaring furred alligators—and I forgot all about my metabolism.

I was hunting with my friend George Papac again, and since he had never hunted black bear before, his was the right of first refusal. George studied the bear for a fair amount of time, then decided he wanted something a little bigger and blacker for his first bear. (And the next afternoon, in fact, George would kill with his eighty-five-pound compound bow a very good, very black six-footer.)

The guide and his assistant had caught all the dogs by then and were holding them on their short chain leads. It was my turn, now, to decide. The bear was fair-sized and nice and fat—he would prove to be a boar—and I knew how succulent the chops and ribs would smell on the slow hardwood heat of a barbecue, and what a pleasure it would be to have some spicy bear salami with Dijon mustard spread on it in a sandwich at lunch on some late-fall day afield.

The bear was now aware that there were men below with the dogs, and he began to rock and sway on the limb where he stood, looking for a way down. Strangely, a cougar will remain placidly treed for an indefinite period as long as a man or dog is standing beneath him, or so it often seems, but it is only a matter of time before a bear will climb down and run again. I looked at him once more, thought of his brown robe laid across my bed, and decided. I slid a 405-grain round into the breech of my Browning 78 single-shot .45-70 and closed the block.

"Take him under his chin," the guide stage-whispered to me.

I put the rifle's crescent butt plate to my shoulder, raised the octagonal barrel, placed the buckhorn sights on the bear's head, and took a deep breath. I waited until his head swung toward me, then shot him under his chin.

The boar bear collapsed on the limb with a shudder and pitched out of the tree. He pinwheeled a hundred feet down to the stream bed and lay there, a wayward nerve firing once or twice in his long-dead body. The dogs were howling madly now as the guide held them back, and the assistant and George and I started down to the bear.

Some say there can't be "much" to hunting bear with hounds—just run one up a tree and shoot it. But the thing about a bear race is that you never know how it will end. You try to hunt bear with your dogs in certain set ways, by riding the strike dog on the hood of your truck down logging roads, or "roading" him, until he winds a scent; by running him down the road ahead of you until he cuts a track; by looking for a fresh track to turn him and the rest of the pack loose on; or by walking him down a canyon where the ground is thick with acorns and the bear are sure to have come to feed. But once the running begins, you just never know *where* or *when* or, especially, *how* it is going to end: whether the bear will tree in the first hundred yards, or run on for ten miles through those impossibly foliated river canyons, pausing only to turn and fight the dogs, who, if you have bred them with sufficient heart, will keep after him all the way, as you keep after them too, hearing all those running voices echoing in the trees—José Ortega y Gasset saw in the hunting with dogs "a certain kind of symphonic majesty."

We had come maybe half to three-quarters of a mile through rough country to reach this bear, and when, in the final fifty feet of the race with the dead bear straight below us, the assistant swung right to go what looked to me to be the long way around, I just kept on going straight until the slope got too steep for me to walk down anymore and I sat and started to slide, then found I could not stop sliding. The assistant turned and saw me and tried to shout, "Not that way!" George was behind me, shouting, *"No,"* and the guide was shouting too, and the dogs were howling, but I was by then airborne.

The cutbank above the rocky edge of the stream was only about twenty feet high, yet it is worth noting how much time a twenty-foot fall gives you for thoughts on the way down. Mine were: Go limp when you land, and I hope I'll be able to climb out afterward. Then I hit and rolled, my head striking something with a sound that reminded me of a time I fired a .50-caliber musket ball into an overripe melon to see what the results would be. I ended up beside the bear, my lovely anachronism of a rifle lying askew in the dirt of the bank, and I remember trying to tell the guide's assistant as he ran up to me—pulling off his T-shirt to press against my head—that everything was all right, as the blood spread out of my hair and began to run down into my face.

You certainly never do know how a bear race is going to end, I thought, when I had stopped bleeding and we were skinning the bear, the dogs lying silently now around us beside the cold water of the stream, waiting for some guts to feed on. Looking up at the long climb ahead, I was glad it had only been my head and not something really important like my legs. So was everybody else.

Remembering Blacktail

Once I was a resident of the state of Oregon, living on its permanently rained-out coast in your basic crab and salmon port (the lumber mill being upriver in the neighboring town). And what that port's citizens did, when they weren't busy fishing or drinking, was hunt blacktail deer on timber company land.

I lived alone above some crumbling sea cliffs in the bottom half of a crumbling duplex. The place had an oil burner and sheets of plastic tacked over the windowpanes, and even with the rent running at about seventy-five per month, it was wildly overpriced. In order to escape my private little slum, therefore, I would occasionally hike across town to the waterfront for a bowl of the best, bar none, clam chowder in the world. My route would invariably carry me past a gas station on the coast highway. In the station's office, behind the giant glass window with a pyramid of silvery motor oil cans stacked in it, hung a set of antlers on a plaque reading "World's Record Columbia Blacktail Deer." I never failed to glance at those antlers, before moving on. When the fall hunting season would come, I would go out to the edge of a clear-cut and sit in the drizzle with my rifle laid across my knees; but I never killed a blacktail deer when I lived in Oregon.

The reason I would no more than glance at that gas station rack as I passed by was perhaps that even the world's record blacktail does not carry what is generally thought of as a "lot of horn," and I was perhaps too green and dumb to appreciate what horn it did carry. Sportsmen who have been weaned on the idea that a deer must bear a striking similarity to such gaudy displays as the "Doug Buris, Jr., Mule Deer Buck" or the "James Jordon Whitetail Buck" before it can be classed as a trophy, tend to overlook the nimble little blacktail. And a peek at the pages of the record book *does* show that any blacktail buck with a spread of as much as twenty inches, hardly wider than the width of his ears, is indeed a highly noteworthy animal. The question is, though: What percentage of blacktail hunters ever bother to take note? One wonders about the number of Boone & Crockett Record Book blacktail racks nailed up as an afterthought to the lintels of cabin and barn doors throughout the coniferous forests of the Pacific Northwest. Or much worse, what number get flipped without a second thought into the trash dumpsters behind butcher shops after the meat's been cut and wrapped?

Despite his smaller rack, the blacktail deer is a mule deer. For the time being, anyway. It is categorized as a subspecies of old *Odocoileus hemionus,* but appears to be on its way to evolving into its own unique brand of deer. Its tail, to be sure, is black, though white underneath with something of a white rim around the lower outside edge. The telling difference, however, between the "blacktail" mule deer and the "muley" mule deer is to be found in as lowly a thing as the metatarsal gland—not even a *real* gland. A muley's metatarsal "gland" is some five inches long and extends almost up to the hock on his rear foot, while on a blacktail it may be only half that length. In average weight a blacktail is appreciably smaller than a muley, and usually smaller than a whitetail. A 150-pound blacktail, even live weight, is *not* a bad deer.

The recognized range of the blacktail runs from Monterey Bay, California, to Kodiak Island, Alaska, and includes some of the most impenetrable rain forest on the surface of the earth. Sasquatch calls this forest home, and they never could find D. B. Cooper and all his hijacked money in it. My grandmother Emma Maude Vaughn McIntyre, born in Iowa in 1886, moved west as the Denver & Rio Grande Railroad carried her stationmaster father west with it, coming in time to Goldfield, Nevada, in the arid heart of the Great Basin desert, a region she dearly loved for its wide-open spaces. There she wed Alfred Samuel McIntyre, who had come out from San Francisco, where he had quit a berth as second mate aboard the *Andrew Welch,* to mine for gold, only to end up working in a mercantile store. In the year of Emma and Alfred's marriage, another of the town's residents, Virgil Earp, died of pneumonia. When in later life my grandmother paid a visit to the Pacific Northwest, she took an immediate hate to it. To her dying day she was pleased to sum up her true feelings about all its ferns and fir trees and tangled wild-berry vines and canopied closeness and eternal wet by cheerfully labeling the entire territory a "green hell."

A person with a kinder view of the place was Theodore Roosevelt, who held that the Columbia blacktail "lives in a land of magnificent timber, where the trees tower far in to the sky, the giants of their kind. . . . There are few more attractive sports than still-hunting on the mountains, among these forests of marvellous beauty and grandeur."

While not in any way doubting the sincerity of those emotions, I do think it is fair to ask just how good the hunting actually was in those "forests of marvellous beauty." I have hunted blacktail deer in "towering" virgin timber, the ground a deep-pile carpet of needles, the light falling like light into the bottom of a well, and I can tell you one thing, blacktail deer don't live there. Blacktail need that combination of feed and cover known as *understory* that develops in open woodlands. They will live off acorns and salal and ferns and moss and even poison oak; they will not live off bare ground.

The best way yet known to create understory is to burn down the forest (do not try this on your own), or by some other means open up the sheltering and smothering overstory. The monumental 1939 Tillamook Fire on the Oregon coast consumed over 300,000 acres of timber. And four years later, when the deer season was reopened, the blacktail numbers were vastly increased and the largest body weights yet known for their subspecies were achieved.

Logging, specifically clear-cutting, which has such a bad name these days in many quarters, is another first-rate method for opening up the forest canopy. As long as you cut in patches or strips, leaving standing timber close by the cleared areas to create the classic model of *edge,* the blacktail will be fruitful and multiply until such time as the second-growth trees mature.

I may have given the impression at the outset that the blacktail is not much sought after for its purely trophy value. That is, of course, not what I meant, merely that its trophy aspect may be sometimes overlooked by those who hunt it for its very fine meat. The blacktail, in fact, is acquiring an ever-widening circle of admirers of its value as a trophy. The genuinely trophy blacktail can, on at least one private ranch in the coastal mountains of Northern California, command a price tag of $2,500. But that is nothing. I once spent $4,000 to take a trophy Sitka blacktail.

This occurred in the fall of 1978, and I had gone brown-bear hunting on Kodiak Island. When I picked up my fifteen-day bear permit at Cy's Sporting Goods in downtown Kodiak, I also purchased a deer tag in case I lucked into a bear early and wanted a reason for staying on a while longer in Alaska. Fifteen days later, with half a hundred bear seen, but none killed, my luck ran out. It seemed.

On the sixteenth day, then, I unfolded that blacktail permit, that relic of my high hopes, from my wallet and set off to fill it. The guide and I had seen any number of blacktail bucks as we sat out on the long shoreline of Uyak Bay, glassing the big white mountains for a sight of a big brown bear. One late evening that November, as

I stood on an outcropping of black rock above the sea where killer whales breached, out of the leafless alders had come a delicate Sitka forked-horn. He seemed rather taller and more graceful than is common among the stocky, almost sheepy Sitka blacktail, and as I stood motionless in the vanishing autumn light, watching him, he advanced across a drained tidal flat toward me. I was curious about how close he would come if I made no movement, and he obliged my curiosity by coming on until he was standing at the base of that black rock, staring up at me from twenty feet away. I stared back. Finally I pulled off my gloves very slowly, then clapped my bare hands together. The buck's ears snapped up and he bounded off, though not with what seemed any great amount of terror. The blacktail of Kodiak Island, where the largest terrestrial eater of meat roams, have, in reality, very little to fear. A bear is almost never fleet enough to capture a deer, unless the deer is very young or very infirm; and until the weather gets nasty enough to drive them from the rugged interior of the island down to the shore, hunters don't get after them much either, especially not in comparison to their large numbers.

On that sixteenth day, then, my guide Bob, the son of the outfitter, the late Park Munsey, and I left from Park's camp in the small diesel cruiser *Kona Wind*, towing a Boston Whaler behind us. The sky was lowering, promising snow. We traveled three or four miles up the bay, to a spot in a protected cove where we anchored the cruiser. Climbing into the Whaler, we started in toward the beach to begin our hunt in the low hills beyond. Only the hunting began before we ever set foot on shore.

I was packing a .458 Winchester Magnum with iron sights on that bear hunt. (Please do not ask why; it *seemed* like the right idea. A .458 is, however, certainly not the weapon of choice for the blacktail-deer hunter. Something in the .243- to .30-caliber range with a good scope is about right, and a professional blacktail guide I know would pick, for what he admits are essentially sentimental reasons, the .257 Roberts as ideal.) As we shoved off from the cruiser and Bob headed the Whaler in, this elephant gun lay peacefully in its canvas case in the bow. Eighty yards off the beach we saw two bucks standing on the water's edge, looking at us come in. As I lunged for my howitzer, barking my shin on the seat, one of the deer sprang away, leaving the other one still looking. I got the gun out and loaded it, and kneeling in the bow of the bobbing open boat, I held the white bead on the buck's chest and fired. Clawing my way back up to the bow after the recoil had rocked me somewhat astern, I saw him still standing, now turned sideways, the big bullet having only shaved the hair along his hip. I worked the bolt again and carefully squeezed off another shot, and this time the deer kicked and took off—took off, I might add, after having been hit by a 510-grain soft-nosed bullet behind the left shoulder!

Dragging the boat up onto the black gravel beach, we trailed him some 150 yards up into a stand of wild roses where he lay dead. He carried a sturdy three-point rack about eighteen inches wide, and we carried him back through the snow that day to feed the camp. Thus the bear hunt became a deer hunt and, not counting the first fifteen days, lasted all of an hour. Not bad for four grand.

At the opposite end of the blacktail's range, in the volcanic foothills between the Cascade Mountains and the Sacramento Valley of California, I once spent a little longer time hunting him, and the merest fraction of the Alaska money. The deer in this country are of the East Tehama herd, the largest single herd in the state, and because at the farthest reaches of their summer range at the crest of the Cascades they may mingle with muleys, they are not recognized by Boone & Crockett as being official blacktail. Yet they are, those metatarsal glands and black tails giving testimony to it.

This is the country where Ishi, the last Yahi Indian and the final "wild" Indian in North America, lived for most of his life, living entirely as a hunter, fisher, and gatherer, living no doubt off these same deer until he was forced down out of his refuge.

In this rocky country of blue oaks and chaparral, it is best to wait till as late in the season as you can to allow the storms of late fall to become your hunting companions. They will, when they come, drive the blacktail down to their traditional wintering grounds, such as those found on the tens of thousands of acres of Dye Creek Preserve. On that land, you can hunt your way out the long ridges that end high above the swiftly running salmon streams that pour down out of the mountains and flow into the Sacramento. Here you may station other hunters out ahead of you and attempt to drive the deer to them. Or you can, where the ridges reach their fingertiplike ends, work above the rimrock and pitch volcanic stones over the edge, hoping to drive out any bedded bucks, and hoping, too, that when they break from cover running you can get a clean shot at them.

This country is also open enough for glassing, but still-hunting can offer the greatest excitement. I still-hunted it one day at the end of October when the late fall storms were something more than companions—more like fierce competitors, or perhaps predators. In the morning, as a storm brewed above me, I worked my way out to the end of a ridge, moving many miles over the ankle-turning lava rocks and through the yellow grass, following a herd of does and fawns on the chance that they would lead me to a buck, or that one would join them. At the ridge's terminus, having not found that buck, having seen many other deer, and having had to tiptoe around a rooting sounder of large wild hogs, I leaned out and looked down into the stream boiling far below me and let the storm break over me.

On the long walk back to the Bronco the rain began to run in clear rivulets through the grass on the ridgetop and lightning cracked over me the entire way, exploding the air near enough to give me a good whiff of ozone as I trudged along, lugging a rifled tube of West German steel, a perfect little lightning rod, across my back. Half a mile from the vehicle, I mounted a rise and saw, water running off my hat brim and into my face, a forked-horn buck with his head down, feeding with a doe and fawn in the rain. I knelt and flipped the covers off my scope. I put the cross hairs on the buck, and what it looked like was the view through the periscope of a U-boat. I studied him for a long while, then slipped the covers back on the scope and stood. The buck saw me and splashed off. I would hunt again the next day.

And that was a day of cold bluebird skies and air. Mike Ballew, Dye Creek's manager, and I were driving up one of the rough ranch roads in the first light when we saw the buck and the doe trotting out in front of us and heading off into some rocks. I got out and, bending low, jogged after them, carrying my .300 held in my right hand. I could make out the two deer disappearing ahead of me into a grove of oaks. On my right side the ground sloped away to a stony creek bed, and on the left an open grassy hill rose up to a high ridge. I went left.

The deer came out of the oaks and started up the hill. The grass was too tall for me to sit or kneel in, so I would have to take an offhand shot. The buck was another forked-horn, maybe a little bigger than the other, but now I wanted my winter's venison far more than I had wanted a set of big horns the day before. I tracked the buck as both deer ran, and then out at two hundred yards he halted and looked back at me as the doe went on. My bullet took him through the spine.

As I walked through the tall grass to his still body, the dew soaking into my boots, I thought of Roosevelt's words about a blacktail he once killed, how he had been "a fine young buck."

We had camped near a little pond, and as evening fell I strolled off toward it and sat down. Just after sunset the buck came out of the woods. For some moments he hesitated and then walked forward and stood by the edge of the water, about sixty yards from me. We were out of meat, so I held right behind his shoulder, and though he went off, his bounds were short and weak, and he fell before he reached the wood.

I wondered, as I came up on my deer, how the antlers had looked on that buck of Roosevelt's, and if Roosevelt had hung them one day at Sagamore Hill. Then I thought how I would like to go back just once more to that Oregon gas station and maybe stand there again in the rain, my hands in my jacket's pockets, staring through the big window and having another look at a world's record.

'Cross Strawberry Creek Mule Deer Liver:
A Recipe

It is for most of us our first memory of venison's taste. It is the venison of deer camps, wood stoves, cold lucent fall nights, a venison that for any number of reasons—as many reasons of sentiment as of perishability—is best eaten while still in that old high lonesome. It can, all by itself, make a trip worthwhile.

To begin with, you cross Strawberry Creek, climb up onto a tall ridge marked by scrub oaks, and kill one mule deer buck. After you have tagged him, dressed him, and hung him well off the ground in a tree, slip his heavy liver into a sack and carry it down through new snow to the cabin of weathered logs. Put up your empty rifle, then blow the cobwebs out of an ancient chipped enamel coffeepot and fill it with icy spring water. Add a fair amount of salt to make the water briny, then place the liver in it. Find a cold shadowed spot, maybe in a snowbank behind the cabin, and let the liver soak, without freezing, for a day. (Make sure the lid is tightly on the pot and it is kept well away from where a badger might wreak havoc on it.) At night, remove the liver from the water and dry it with a clean yellow towel. Peel all the thin bluish membrane from the organ's surface and with your sharp skinning knife cut slices 1/3 inch thick. In a heavy iron skillet with a blackened bottom, lightly brown slices of onion in bacon fat, then remove them and set aside, keeping them warm. Into white flour mix salt and pepper, to taste, in a plastic bag that used to hold a loaf of bread, and shake the slices of liver in it, flouring each evenly. Spoon more bacon fat from the red Folger's can and add it to the skillet until the fat is 1/4 inch deep and very hot, though not smoking. Now place the slices in the hot fat and fry quickly. Turn the meat when beads of blood begin to appear on the white top side. When the liver is done, the flour coating should be crisp and the meat slightly pink inside, not gray as an aged pronghorn's tongue! Put the meat on a platter of cracked blue china, place the warm onions on top, get the old men to turn the ball game down on the radio, tell the gin rummy players to clear their Bicycle cards off the table, and set the meat before them. Serve with fried potatoes, a salad of fresh iceberg lettuce and wedges of tomatoes, perhaps some hot garlic bread, cold milk, and drop of whiskey. Cut a piece with the same knife you've been using for everything else so far this trip and lift the fork to your mouth. As you pause a second for the liver to cool, smelling its warm dark smell, look to the cabin window slicing and polishing the night as if it were the quarried face of some unlimited deposit of obsidian butting up against the cabin. Wonder if it has begun to snow again out there in the black, and take your time with this meal. It's what you came for.

Winter Is a Greater Hunter
Than Man Will Ever Be

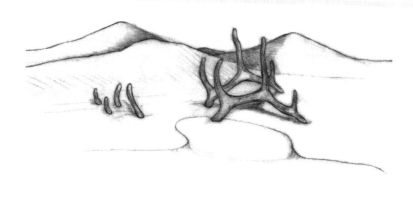

At least northwest Colorado was *prettier* that fall than the hunter could ever remember seeing it. The hills were patched in lime and rust and khaki and red and in yellows ranging from lemon to gold. The whitetail jackrabbits, already whitening for winter—while the hunter paraded in state-required clothing the color of a campfire—were big as Persian cats. Mountain bluebirds fluttered on the tips of twigs, and the dark silhouettes of eagles sailed beneath the blue sky.

At night the hunter stood outside the cabin with a puddle of sour mash in the bottom of his cup and looked up at Polaris, Draco, the Pleiades, the powdery smudge of the Milky Way, the Squaw and the Papoose blinking in the Big Dipper, and all the other stars whose names he had never learned. He heard coyotes near him at night, but could not see them in the day. When he set out hunting at dawn, he found the fresh tracks of voles, ruffed grouse, the little-bear ones of badgers. Among the shimmering aspens the elk tracks were very thick. An old Basque shepherd wearing handmade Mexican spurs told the hunter that he was seeing elk these days in places he had never seen them before. Last September his youngest boy, who was out herding with him before going back to college, had been drawn to a ridgetop by the sound of early morning bugling and had counted thirty-five elk in the small meadow below. Lot of elk in the country, the shepherd concluded. What there were not a lot of, however, in this country above Meeker, Colorado, were the mule deer the hunter had come seeking. For the first year in the five that he had been coming here, the hunter would not carry a buck home when he left.

It was not easy to explain. The season before had been good. The seven of them in the camp had taken seven bucks off the 2,500 acres and had passed up as many more. They had returned to Southern California and spent the winter with venison in their freezers, antlers on their walls, and expectations of even better things to come next year in their heads. And while rain fell on Southern California, snow fell on Colorado.

When word of this Colorado winter reached the hunter, his mind—refusing to accept the fact that Nature herself was capable of tearing down the hunting—chose to confine all the bad weather to the Gunnison area. That region was mentioned in all the reports as being hardest hit, and it was nowhere near Meeker. That spring, for instance, when the hunter came upon the following curious item in the paper, it only helped to confirm his peculiar notion—because the reservoir in question was near there—that winter must have overlooked everywhere in Colorado *except* Gunnison:

> *A wildlife tragedy in Colorado: 62 elk drowned in Blue Mesa Reservoir last winter. Two piles of dead elk, 50 yards apart, were found May 6 when the reservoir was lowered.*
>
> *A state biologist, after examining the size of fetuses in cows, estimated the elk fell through the ice in early December. Twenty-nine of the dead elk were pregnant cows.*

No one, it seems, has explained what the elk were seeking on that ice.

But the snow came down northwest of Meeker as well, came down heavy enough to bury all the sagebrush and make it impossible for the mule deer to paw through it. As the deer starved they foundered in the drifts, too weak to move or to defend themselves. So the coyotes, usually so wary of deer, came. Weighing no more than the weight of fur and teeth and hunger, they were able to run on top of the frozen crust. To deer already dying of starvation, such coyotes were a kindness, and by spring there was talk of 200,000 dead animals.

All through that winter, while it rained in Southern California and snowed in Colorado, the hunter had been telling his friend Tom Davis about the place where they would hunt in the fall. Telling him? *Regaling* him was more like it. It would be Tom's first season in camp, and he wanted to know everything. The hunter obliged by first telling him that the town of Meeker was named for Nathan C. Meeker, who in 1869 left the editorial staff of Horace Greeley's New York *Tribune* and, following his former employer's famous advice, went west—albeit, at age fifty-two, hardly as a young man. His subsequent career in the Colorado Territory proved at best checkered—at worst fatal. A strict teetotaler, Meeker succeeded in founding the temperance colony of Greeley, while never succeeding at making one thin dime from anything he turned his hand to. In 1878 he was finally granted the boon of being named agent to the White River Ute Reservation and bungled that badly enough to start the Ute War of 1879, and to get himself and every one of the agency's male employees massacred at a site five miles outside the present town that bears his name. In later, less bellicose days Theodore Roosevelt came to Meeker to follow the hounds and in 1901 killed a cougar that was the world's record for sixty-three years, and still stands No. 3 in the book. As far as the hunter was concerned, the next exciting event to take place in Meeker occurred when a 350-pound Texan, dried blood still on his Lone Star hands, stamped back into the El Rancho Cocktail Lounge one deer-season afternoon, wanting to know who, *exactly,* had stolen the five-point buck he'd left outside in his Jeep. There was, to be sure, a high old time to be had in that saloon for a spell.

This sort of information didn't satisfy Tom's thirst for knowledge, however. He wanted to know the specifics of the place where he was going to hunt. What sort of terrain would it be? What kind of weather should he expect? What time did shooting light come? The hunter answered to the best of his ability, telling Tom in the process about all the deer he had seen in all the years past, the long shots made across steep canyons, and the bucks he had lucked into, the gangs of elk crossing the meadows at first light, the sage grouse, as big as turkeys, exploding from cover right under his feet, the dry days, the wet ones, the ones with snow. But that still left Tom to agonize all spring and summer over what rifle to carry, what weight bullets to load, what kind of shoes to wear. He settled at last on a Mag-Na-Ported .30-'06 BAR throwing 180-grain Nosler partition bullets. On his feet he would lace Adidas in warm weather and insulated pacs in cold. He meant to be prepared.

By early October, however, when they were packing to leave, Tom and the hunter and Roy and Charley Spiller and Bob and Dave and Manuel—despite all their preparedness and false hopes—could no longer ignore the persistent reports of massive die-off. This season could not be like the last. And yet, in some ultimate, metaphysical, grand-scheme-of-things sense, what the hell difference did that make? The hunter was put in mind of the closing passage of E. Douglas Branch's classic *The Hunting of the Buffalo:*

> *And it is only 30 years ago {1900} that a band of Indians . . . saddled their ponies and rode away—"as of old, but in silence and sadness."*
>
> *"Where are you bound?" some white man asks; and they answer, "For the buffalo."*
>
> *"But there are no more."*
>
> *"No, we know it."*
>
> *"Then why are you going on such a foolish chase?"*
>
> *"Oh, we always go at this time; maybe we shall find some."*

While the mule deer had in no way met with the bisons' fate—nor would ever meet with anything even remotely like it—the hunter could see that the odds that fall would not be with him and the others. Yet each fall there was still something—something in the blood, let's say—that compelled him and the men he hunted with always to go onto the Colorado Plateau at this time; and bad winter or no—perhaps, even, mule deer or no—that something would not leave the blood.

They reached camp the Friday morning before the season opened. The hunter took Tom out that afternoon to show him the lay of the land. As they kept beneath the ridgelines and crept through the groves of scrub oak, as they glassed across the canyons and searched the ground for deer sign, they soon knew that winter *had* set its mind to it. For two hours they still-hunted without rifles. They did not see a living deer, found no more than one or two beds, heard almost no sound.

"Probably not even any of those sage grouse left," Tom ventured, just before an entire covey rose up like an atomic mushroom cloud in front of them and whirred far out over the coppery sageland. Something, at least, had made it through. They went on.

As they walked, the bones lay around them like spilled dominoes in the yellow grass. The smooth tines of the antlers rose symmetrically above the polished caps of skulls, the herbivorous jaws set in permanent rictus. There wasn't enough meat on the skeletons for the ants to bother with.

The hunter tried to show Tom the best place to hunt in the morning—knowing full well it would not make one ounce of difference, but knowing, too, that you always had to try. He showed Tom, also, the canyon where their friend Charley had killed his first buck and then did not know how to dress him. After some searching, Charley found Roy, the man who had taught the hunter and almost everybody else the hunter knew how to dress a deer, and negotiated a contract with him whereby, in exchange for Roy's merely *showing* him how to clean his deer, Charley would clean Roy's when he shot it—providing, of course, that Charley was in the vicinity at the time. Roy agreed to the terms and followed Charley to his buck. Charley was stripping the alimentary canal from the carcass, per Roy's instructions, when Roy glanced across canyon, whispered to Charley not to bother wiping off his knife, put down his pipe, lifted his .243, and killed one of the biggest bucks any of them had seen in years. Of the hundreds of deer Roy had shot since he was a boy, he could not recall killing one at a more opportune moment.

That was one story about the place that the hunter knew how to tell Tom, but there were others he did not know how to tell. As they slanted their way down off a high ridge, the hunter did not know how to tell Tom about the way Old Mac had hunted this ridge his last time out when he was seventy-five and everybody was afraid he was going to die on them. But when those who had been on that hunt met again at Old Mac's funeral two years later, all they could talk about was how good he had done that last time. Old Mac had been a tough one, but now the hunter didn't know how to tell that to Tom, who had never known the man. Nor did the hunter know how to tell him about the way they had come here after the other area they had hunted for so many years had gone bad when the owner let anyone willing to pay onto it; and it became like hunting in a Boy Scout jamboree or trying to fish the bank of a stocked stream on opening morning—there had been enough blaze orange in sight to create a false dawn. Tom simply would have had to have been there to understand, and he hadn't been. Not even attempting to tell him these stories, the hunter told Tom they should head in now.

Four days later the hunter sat in the kitchen of the cabin, playing a game of muggins with Roy, the white dominoes spilled like bones on the tabletop. The light dropped through the holes the snow and pack rats had made in the ceiling, and the air in the kitchen hummed with flies and yellow jackets. As the hunter played, he was trying to guess where he should hunt next, having hunted every likely spot on the property at least twice in the last four days. That was when the Basque shepherd rode up and knocked on the door. Entering, he accepted a beer and sat down to tell Roy and the hunter about the elk and the mule deer and coyotes and "snow up to here" and the winter. The shepherd did not hunt much these days, but he loved seeing the deer around him when he tended his flocks. He believed the state ought to close the deer hunting for at least three years to give the herds time to build back up, that the state should bring in proper feed for the deer in the bad winters, and that somebody had to do something about these coyotes.

The hunter nodded at it all. He felt inadequate to argue against the beliefs of this man who had lived out on the land more than the hunter ever would, who saw the mule deer every day—in migration, in mating, in birth, and in dying—when the hunter saw them only a few days out of the year. If he tried to explain, using scientific logic and statistical data, that men and coyotes probably killed no more mule deer than a few weeks in January would anyway, he knew it would ring false, not only to this shepherd but to himself as well. So he nodded. When the shepherd shook hands and jangled out in his spurs, the hunter thought: Yeah, maybe we don't have any business being out here, maybe it *ought* to be closed down; but where would I go, come next fall?

The hunter finished his game of dominoes; then, realizing there was no sense to wasting what hunting time he had left, he slung his rifle over his shoulder and started out on his own "foolish chase." Tom was already out, having taken off at dawn and come in at dark every day of the hunt, intending to stay out until, like those Indians, he "found some." That was a good sign to the hunter; it meant that no matter how this year turned out, and no matter how grim the prospects looked for next year, as long as Tom could come back and hunt, he would; and the hunter would be assured of having someone to join him in the fall.

As the hunter walked, he believed he could nearly be content out here with just the sun-warmed ground to put his feet on and the clouds shaped like sage grouse wings in the sky to see. Heading up a far canyon at the end of the property, he found a good seat in a fragrant bed of sagebrush partway up a hill. The hunter had thus far tried stalking for game, glassing for it, and spooking it out of cover by charging like a tormented warlock through the scrub oak groves. Now he would put to the test the age-old technique of just plain sitting. He sat there till sunset. He stared at the hills and trees and brush until they all began staring back at him. Then he stood and started home.

The hunter saw the mule deer as he was passing a side canyon running off the one he had been sitting in. The buck was five hundred yards away, moving toward the ridge. As soon as the hunter spotted him holding his rack-laden head high and walking with the grace only big bucks acquire, he sank to his hands and knees and began crawling through the sage toward the animal. When the hunter reached an old weathered fence post, he slowly rose and steadied his .300 on it. The buck had halted just beneath the ridgeline and seemed to be looking back at him. There was good light left, and the hunter had the cross hairs anchored to the top of the deer's sleek-coated shoulder. As his finger lay on the trigger, he was able in his mind to see the entire progression: the exhale, the recoil, the buck coming down like a collapsing scaffold.

The hunter would climb up and, unable to resist, would lift the head and hold the polished antlers in his hands a moment. Then he would swing the deer's tail downhill and roll him onto his back. When he opened the animal, he would marvel at the layer of pearly fat that would have carried this buck through the most determined winter. In the cold October evening, he would notice the heat rising off the flesh and have to remind himself again of the good taste of fresh liver at breakfast and how delicious the chops would be in a rainy Southern California February when the snow would be five feet deep in Colorado. And while the hunter saw all this in his mind, he just watched the buck turn and let him continue on to the jagged ridge, climbing unhurriedly until he topped out and ambled into the approaching night.

As the hunter found his way back to camp, he met Tom in the darkness. Tom had not seen a buck all day, but was nonetheless delighted by sightings of numerous does and fawns—delighted, in fact, by the simple act of *being* Out There. The hunter wondered if he knew how to tell Tom about what had just happened and that when men, unlike winter, hunted, their hearts could carry away more than their hands.

After turning it over for a minute, the hunter decided: *Hell,* Tom knows that already. He's been here.

Not a Goose Story

Jim Latta and I have been wading this beaver marsh all morning. The long marsh grass is bent by frost, and there is ice in my mustache and my feet feel good and cold in my hip boots. So far we have jumped maybe half a dozen ducks. Jim has managed to kill one teal; I've managed to fire not even a shot. Which is fine.

The dense morning fog has begun to lift by the time we have meandered across the marsh and come to stand on the bank of the New Fork, watching it run clear and chill with deep pools holding brown trout. Jim starts to move on but then points into a stand of cottonwoods on the other side of the river. I look where he's aimed his finger and see the brown hillock of a Shiras moose cow rising up among the trees.

"She's one big old cow," Jim says admiringly. "You kill her back in there, though," he adds, sinking off once more into the marsh, "the only way you're getting her out's with a knife and fork."

Jim lives at the foot of the Wind Rivers. The view from his living room soars up and away forever to shining peaks. There are sheep and elk back in there, and moose, antelope, mule deer, ducks, geese, and trout down here. Here and there are bears.

I met Jim, and his brother-in-law Jim Wise, and Wise's brother Jerry, once down in the Caribbean. They had gone there to fish and hunt and have a good time for themselves; I had gone to see if there was anything to be written about it. I go to many places to see what there is to be written about them, making what passes for my "living" telling others what I have seen. Sometimes the going can get to be *too* much of a good thing, though, as in this October when I find myself between terminals, between one too many jet aircraft and those places I have to go to make a living—with even more of the same ahead of me—so that *this* October comes to look more like that "damp, drizzly November in my soul" than the *dandy* early fall it ought to be. I have a little time in the vale between the terminals, however, time enough to go someplace and do some things whose only recommendation for me is that it's where *I* want to go and what *I* want to do. Going whaling is pretty much out, of course, but I *can* go to Wyoming. And not have to tell a soul.

That is why Jim and I are slogging around in this essentially aqueous solution of the Cowboy State on this frigid morning, trying to frighten assorted members of the family Anatidae into headlong flight so we may kill and eat them. And the best part is this: no one told me to come here; I don't have to tell anybody what I have seen; I am here to find no "angle"; my only reason for being here is because it is where, *precisely,* I want to be today.

So we go on crossing ponds behind the dams of beavers and sink to the tops of our waders in green bogs, have mallards we are trying to put a sneak on vanish into the thin air and watch plumes of steam rise off the river like the breaths of a hundred men, with absolutely no ulterior motive. As we are heading back to the truck, we see a pair of honkers beating away from us in the blue sky, and I think happily: There goes the *goose* story; *vaya con Dios!* As we put up our unloaded guns, Jim is downright apologetic about the shooting. He needn't be; I am also *doing* precisely what I want.

We drive on down to the Green River where it runs beneath high cliffs at the back of Jim's wife's family's ranch. As we bounce across the bottomland, we see jacksnipe and four-point mule deer bucks. Jim has high hopes for the fishing, wanting to show me a good time. (Jim, I'm having it.) But when we reach the river it is an unseasonable two feet too high and cloudy as dishwater. We stand on the rocky bank under the warm fall sun, our spinning rods dangling listlessly. Then, as we go on standing, a raft of one dozen Canada geese floats placidly around the bend like carefree river holidayers and rams smack into us. We gawk at them clamoring and flapping over our heads, their bellies seeming close enough for us to brush our fingertips over the down, the shotguns securely back up in the pickup. (I told you, I want to shout at them, there will be no *goose* story!) We begin to fish.

We make long, vain casts into the current. Moving upriver, we slather across the slick stony bottom but find, everywhere, the news is the same. Jim the Wyoming lad is used to running water that lies between the banks of a river as limpidly as if a crack squad of world-class glaziers had puttied it into place and polished it to spotlessness with vast white cotton hankies. He's also used to a mess of trout, *right now*. Me, I'm used to nothing of the sort. When Jim sees a river as unnaturally high and muddy green and basically unfishable as this one is in *October* of all months, he quite rightly trudges out of it after three casts and reclines upon the nearest gravel bar, idly flicking over smooth pebbles with his index finger. Me, I go on standing in the river, flicking out my sparkling lure that was made in France, neither killing time nor injuring eternity, just trying to get as much out of this deal as I can. In a while, though, to make Jim feel better, I pretend I am disappointed, too, and leave the river behind.

Later, Jim and I fish a jeweled string of tiny beaver ponds that hold cutthroat. Only not today. Which, again, is fine. After all, this is going to be between just me and nobody else.

The canyon where the ponds lie coiled ascends to snow and is garnished at its foot with aspens just now starting to turn. We break down our rods and head back in the pickup. Then in the last beaver pond, just on the far side of the aspens, we see a flock of young mallards. We stalk them like quail. They rise off the water and head quacking out over the sage and I down one for my three shots while Jim neatly takes three for his. They are too few to make any kind of *real* duck story, but are fat and warm in our hands and will be as tasty as all get-out.

Afterward, in the Eagle Bar in La Barge, a time-honored saloon very much in the glorious middle of just about nowhere—a saloon built of antique wood, patronized by even *more* antique cowpokes, and decorated with a water-stained print on the wall depicting the gallant (and addlepated) Last Stand of George Armstrong Custer and the men of the Seventh, a print that must have been hot off the presses mere weeks after the incident—Jim and I sit on stools and sip a beer, our waders turned down like seven-league boots and spattered with duck blood, the cleaned birds lying cool outside in a fishing creel. Some coot who tells us he's spent his life in a "kerosene orchard" leans against the bar beside me in a pose that looks like that famous one of Proust's (if the elegant Marcel had taken to wearing a sweaty old Stetson, going about Paris in need of a shave, and leaving most of his teeth at home, soaking in a glass), and asks where I got the red Police Braces holding up my green woolen britches. Grand Junction, Colorado, I answer, remembering with some pride the exact cloudy day a decade ago when I had also gone hunting solely for the sake of *going hunting*.

"Colorado's where I'm from, too," he says, seeming to tip me the wink on some secret, then drifting off down the bar. Jim and I finish our beers and start to leave, but the barmaid, unbidden, brings us a couple of fresh ones.

"What," we ask, "is this?"

She points to a tall fellow framed by the waning sun pouring through the big front window, a fellow adazzle in white dry-cleaned Western wear, pumping hands and slapping backs for all he's worth. "Just bought the house a round. I think he's *running* for something," she confides with a shrug.

"But I don't even *live* in Wyoming," I confess.

"That's okay, honey. Just drink your beer. I won't breathe a word."

Four days and one two-day blizzard of horizontally propelled snow later, I am south of Rawlins, hunting pronghorns with the Wise brothers. And, I think with a wicked thrill, this is one story with no deadline. We are *all* out here now just trying our damnedest to have a good time, and I don't *ever* have to breathe a word of it to anyone. There are times, I tell myself, when I *must* lay eyes on a shining mountain, or cast a line into a running river, or try to touch a wild goose, or chase an antelope on the prairies for no better reason than that all those things are out there, somewhere, to be done, and something within me, something that *is* me, sends me out to do them. This seems like one of those times, and I'm never going to tell anyone about it.

It's being a roamer, I say to myself, turning up the collar of your coat and turning your back on the "world" as you sail away. Yet most every wayfarer returns, and what Ishmael is without his tale to tell? I begin, dimly, to realize something then, that what makes me go out also makes me have to tell of what I have seen once I come back. The two are bound in such a way in me that it is *not* that I have to tell of the sights I've seen in order to make my living; in far too real a sense, I have to tell of them to *live*. I see that by raw nature I am a teller of tales, a tattler if you like. I should have been the coot who worked not in the kerosene orchard, but by sitting on the rock behind the fire at night a hundred centuries ago, telling how it was the last time the mammoths passed this way. I remember now, almost sadly—but not quite—that so far I have been unable to keep even *one* secret in this world.

Anyway, out here hunting pronghorn is about as good a time and place as any to come to such an understanding of oneself, I do see. Therefore, with not a little newfound humility, I wish to tell you, if I may, how in an interval of snow-brightened light between the shadows of two airplane terminals, I once upon a time saw a great herd of antelope run along the rocky floor of a wide canyon, then start to turn up to the high ground where I waited. There was a big buck, his long horns black as ebony wood, bringing up the rear; and as he galloped onto the top of the ridge, I raised my rifle . . .

The Long Hunt

The beginning was in a time of ice, perhaps as much as forty thousand years ago. It began when hunters from Siberia, trailing herds of caribou and bison and mastodon, crossed the land bridge of Beringia—now covered once more by the sea—and discovered a continent populated only by animals. If a date for when it ended is needed, then August 29, 1911, is as good a one as any.

At dawn on that day a Yahi Indian—the last living member of his tribe, the last "wild" Indian in North America—having been driven by starvation and loneliness to abandon his hunter's life in the rugged volcanic Lassen country of northeastern California, was found huddled in the corral of a slaughterhouse near the Sacramento Valley town of Oroville. The Indian wore thongs of deer hide through the lobes of his ears and a wooden peg through his nose and had his black hair singed close to his head in a sign of mourning. For all the fifty-some years of his life, while the other native hunters of America were systematically put off the land and saw the game destroyed, he had lived, with the steadily dwindling handful of his tribe, hidden from the sight of the nineteenth-century civilization that warred, through ignorance, on his people at every turn. He managed during those years to live the same hunter's life the Yahi had practiced for the thousands of years they dwelt in their tiny, nearly inaccessible nation. It was only when a party of surveyors from the Oro Light & Power Company, searching for a suitable place to run a power line (to run, in fact, the modern world) across that country, stumbled onto his hidden camp and, while from concealment he watched, removed in a gesture of gross stupidity his bow and arrows and salmon harpoon and all the other implements of his survival for their "souvenirs," it was only then that he was no longer able to carry on that life.

His name, the name he was given by the White Men because, following Indian custom, he would never reveal his true name to strangers, was Ishi—in his own tongue, "man." Excited scientists from the University of California swiftly claimed Ishi as their ward, dressed him in new clothes, and fetched him back to San Francisco to live in the Museum of Anthropology there so they might learn from him the ways of a hunter unchanged by civilization. Ishi proved a great boon to those scientists.

Aside from the knowledge gained from him, however, much information has now been gathered about the various ways of the North American Indian hunters who preceded Ishi. By around 10,000 B.C., it is known from archaeological findings, those once-Siberian hunters had armed themselves with fluted stone spearpoints and were able, very effectively, to hunt down the largest mammal ever to roam this continent, the mammoth. This ancient elephant stood sometimes fourteen feet tall, and to comprehend the daring of its hunter, stand sometime yourself beside the rearticulated skeleton of one in a museum. Now, as you gaze upward at the gigantic skull and the huge curving tusks of ivory, imagine this creature is alive and imagine, too, that all you carry in your hand is a length of stick with a piece of chipped rock bound by animal sinew to its end. Yet men armed in just this fanciful fashion could, in relatively small bands, regularly attack and kill a herd of mammoths and feed themselves and their women and children and aged for weeks on the prize.

At the same time they hunted elephants, these first Americans, or Paleo-Indians as science knows them, hunted as well the several species of bison that also abounded. Then around 8000 B C , for reasons not yet understood, all the megafauna such as elephant and ground sloth and all but one of the bison species were gone, utterly, leaving that sole remaining species of buffalo, *Bison bison,* called by one writer "the grandest ruminant in nature," to become the grandest quarry of the American chase.

Until the advent of the horse in the sixteenth century, the killing of the buffalo was a mass communal exercise for the Indian hunter. One method he used was merely to encircle a herd with a sufficient number of men and spear the bison to death. Another called for him to drive the animals into a natural or constructed pound and kill them there, while still another involved his ringing them with fire but leaving a gap for their escape and slaying them as they fled the flames. The most spectacular method used, though, may have been the buffalo jump, or *piskun.* Here armed runners would surround a herd and drive it over a cliff or into an arroyo where other hunters would be waiting at the bottom to finish off any beasts that survived the fall.

These hunters probably did not have the luxury of stopping to count how many buffalo they were doing in or to limit their kill to the precise number they could butcher and carry off. Finding fresh meat was a high-risk venture; and when there was a need, one took the opportunity to kill game whenever that opportunity was fortuitously presented. Beneath the mountain of flesh at the bottom of any buffalo jump would always be buried dead animals that could not be gotten to. These had to be left to rot, and they would probably be looked upon by the hunter as a handy form of oblation.

Those buffalo in the pile that could be gotten to, however, would be dealt with according to strict rules of procedure. They would immediately be rolled off onto their bellies and skinned down the back, the hide peeled off and used as a clean mat for laying the cuts of meat on. The first meat stripped away would be the tender "blanket of flesh" from just under the hide. Next would be removed the forelegs and shoulder blades, then the highly regarded hump meat. By now it would be possible for the Indian hunter to cut into the body cavity with his flint or bone knife, and such succulent viands as the still-hot internal organs offered would be dined on, as it were, alfresco. The fresh raw tongue might also be enjoyed at this time.

After the remaining hindquarters, head, and neck were butchered out, the meat would be carried back to the band's encampment and divided according to a prescribed order, the hunter who struck the first blow receiving the animal's hide along with his select cut of meat, the one who first touched the dead animal receiving another portion, and so on until everyone, hunter and nonhunter alike, was provided for. The feasting could then begin.

An Indian hunter could eat between ten and twenty pounds of fresh meat a day during a feast, consuming along with it pieces of fat like so much bread. What could not be eaten fresh was dried in the sun, then some of the jerky would be made into pemmican by grinding it between stones and mixing it with dried berries and fat (in the case of the more preferred "sweet pemmican," this fat would be derived by boiling the marrow out of the broken buffalo bones). Compressed and packed into rawhide bags and kept away from moisture, this meat could last up to five years.

Besides meat, of course, the buffalo provided the Indian hunter with nearly every item he used in daily life. The Indian made his bed from the thick buffalo hide of winter—when he could go alone or in a small party across the top of the snow on snowshoes and catch the bison trapped in the drifts—and the hide of a heifer killed in late fall made the finest of robes. Hides from summer kills, when the hair was thin, were best for dressing and turning into tipis, clothes, shields, packs, bags, ropes, snowshoes, and boat covers. Buffalo sinew made bowstrings and sewing thread. Horns made spoons and cups, and the scalp and horns made the medicine man's "buffalo cap." Hair was woven into reatas and belts. Glue was made from hooves and the shavings from bull hides. The paunch could ingeniously be turned into a disposable—and edible—stew kettle. And the buffalo's dried "chips" made many fine fires. As many as eighty-seven nonfood uses of the buffalo by the Indian have been recorded, and it can be said that all of the buffalo he *could* carry away from the kill was put to good use. This fundamental relationship between the buffalo and the Indian who hunted him—"All the animal gives to me, I will put to good use," the Indian seemed to say—in fact, between the Indian hunter and *all* the game he pursued remained remarkably unaltered down through the millennia until the great herds' final days of existence.

Another relationship that remained mostly unaltered throughout the Indian's history as a hunter was that of the very *nature* of hunting to him. Hunting to the Indian was not a sporting proposition; he did not do it for the "fun" of it. This is not to say that he could not enjoy what was, to him, his work—there are far worse ways of making a living than by hunting game—but it *is* to say that that is exactly what hunting was to him: work. His job, plain and simple. And in the case of trying to kill a large, dangerous animal, a moose or a bison or an elk or a bear or even a deer, with a spear or an arrow or maybe just a club, it was a particularly *tough* job indeed. So it seemed merely good sense to him that he should kill only when he needed something to eat or wear, and should not do so wantonly at the risk of depleting the game and thereby making his job just that much harder. When these relationships began to break down was when the White Men came and could offer the Indian hunter "things"—whiskey, steel knives and tomahawks, textiles, trade rifles (and, as a sort of lagniappe, alcoholism, syphilis, smallpox, and measles) in exchange for the fur and hides and tongues of animals. Then more than a few Indians proved they could slaughter with quite as much gusto as any white "buffalo runner" or the worst *wah-kéitcha* (an Indian term for a French-Canadian trapper, meaning "bad medicine") in some fur company's employ.

Yet this anomie did not come about until the forced end of the Indian's long hunt in America, and before that time there is little evidence that, as long as he was hunting for subsistence, he ever posed a serious threat to any animal species. He did, however, have a phenomenally lethal knowledge of the ways of animals and of deadly methods for drawing them to him.

As modern archers know, it is no easy task to still-hunt game with a bow, and hunting from a stand is a far more successful technique. The Indian hunter long knew this and became a master of concealment and decoy. He would wait in cover along a game trail and, wearing an animal-skin mask or an entire animal head or hide, would imitate the sounds of large and small game: bird calls of all kinds, a kissing noise to attract rabbits, calling on a turkey's wing bone to entice a gobbler, blowing on a leaf reed held in the hands to mimic a fawn's whimper and draw in a doe, trumpeting for caribou and moose with a piece of rolled bark, pouring water from a container into a stream or lake to imitate a cow moose urinating and get a rutting bull's attention, antler rattling for bucks, striking stones or sticks together to sound like bighorn rams fighting. He would also rig up nets and snares to drive small game and antelope and deer, and even elk, into. (One report has the Pilgrim Fathers walking into the woods shortly after their arrival and being hoisted up in Indian deer snares.) Under the skin of a white wolf an Indian could crawl into a bison herd with his bow and make a kill. And when all else failed for the Shoshoni hunter, he would take off on foot and simply *run* a pronghorn to death.

An Indian hunter's weapons were the tools of his trade, and they were as valuable to him as his tools are to any craftsman—the Indian hunter being very much a craftsman of the hunt and the kill. For small game and birds he had slings and, in the South, blowguns. The hand spear was among the earliest of his big-game weapons. In open country, or with exceptionally wary game, a device for extending the hunter's range was needed, and petroglyphs found in the deserts of Utah and California show Anasazi hunters, the people the Navajo knew as "the ancient ones," bringing down sheep using darts hurled from throwing sticks called *atlatls*. But with its development, the bow became the most universally used weapon.

The highest-quality bows were fabricated from slices of horn and bone—with elk antler held to make the finest bows—glued together, then rubbed and filed down and wrapped with sinew. With painting and ornamenting, a first-rate hunting bow could require three months of labor to complete. For wooden bows Osage orange, called *bois d'arc* by the voyageurs, was widely considered the best material, though almost any wood would do in a pinch, since it was usually submitted to the same cutting and gluing process as horn. (For his part, Ishi made his bows from a single seasoned branch of mountain juniper that he cut and bent to shape and backed with sinew parchment he affixed to the bow with a glue made from boiling the skins of salmon.) Until the introduction of the light, short-barreled Winchester repeating carbine in 1873, the Indian hunter felt much better served by his bow, and reports of his shooting an arrow completely through a bison or of being able to fire one arrow in a high arc and then get off half a dozen more shots before the first shaft touched the ground help to explain why.

Arrow shafts were cut from the shoots of such wood as serviceberry and gooseberry and cherry in late winter when the sap was down and the sticks would not split while drying. The cured shafts were sanded to a uniform diameter by passing them between two grooved pieces of sandstone and were straightened by first rubbing them with fat and then heating them. Then various bone or stone or wood tools and wrenches, or sometimes only the arrow maker's own hands, were employed to make the shafts true; and they were then scored with grooves along their lengths, said to be put there to let the blood flow freely from the wound. Oddly, the art of making stone arrowheads seems to have been a lost one to the Plains Indians of the eighteenth and nineteenth centuries. (Ishi could make them from obsidian, and he showed the scientists studying him what an exacting and exhausting chore it was to chip a point out of the black glass of a volcano.) The Indians of the Plains made most of their arrowheads out of the iron they found in the metal hoops of barrels and the bottoms of frying pans abandoned by, or taken from, westering pioneers.

If the most widely distributed weapon among the Indian hunters was the bow, the finest weapon they possessed was the one the Conquistadores had bequeathed them, the horse. As the wild herds of mustangs spread north through the Plains during the sixteenth and seventeenth centuries, the Indian of that region became several new things. He became the best light cavalryman the world would ever know; he became a true nomad; and he became, by himself, a hunter of formidable talent. He no longer had to depend on drives or other near-military campaigns to acquire meat. With his long buffalo lance, a lone horseman could pick out the running game he wanted, spear it behind its last rib or slash its hamstring, then ride on after another animal, sure that his first prey was down. To better suit it to firing from horseback, his bow had to be shortened, to forty inches or less, and the Indian hunter learned to wield that abbreviated bow with supreme accuracy.

An early witness to the Plains Indian's prowess as a mounted predator was George Catlin. He was a Pennsylvanian, an indifferent lawyer, an accomplished hunter, and a mostly self-taught painter who saw the Indian with a vision unclouded by cant or romanticism at a time when the Indian was still relatively untouched by the spreading influence of American culture. As a young girl, his mother had been taken captive in an Indian raid, and the stories she filled his boyhood with about her life among the Red Men so marked Catlin that he would find himself journeying west, summer after summer, into the country of the Sioux and Pawnee and Comanche for most of the decade of the 1830s so that, in his own words, he might rescue "from oblivion the looks and customs of the vanishing race of native man in America." (Wounded Knee was still sixty years away, but even at that remove, Catlin could still see how numbered were the free-roaming Indian's days.)

Writing in his two-volume *Letters and Notes on the Manners, Customs, and Condition of the North American Indians,* Catlin gives us a vivid picture of the Indian hunter and his horse in their prime:

> *The Indian . . . mounted on his little wild horse, which has been through some years of training, dashes off at full speed amongst the herds of buffaloes, elks, or even antelope, and deals his deadly arrows to their hearts from his horse's back. The horse is the fleetest animal of the prairie, and easily brings his rider alongside of his game, which falls a certain prey to his deadly shafts, at the distance of a few paces.*
>
> *In the chase of the buffalo, or other animal, the Indian generally*

*"strips" himself and his horse, by throwing off his shield and quiver, and
every part of his dress, which might be an encumbrance to him in running;
grasping his bow in his left hand, with five or six arrows drawn from his
quiver, and ready for instant use. . . .*

*These horses are so trained, that the Indian has little use for the rein,
which hangs on the neck, whilst the horse approaches the animal on the right
side, giving his rider the chance to throw his arrow to the left; which he does at
the instant when the horse is passing—bringing him opposite to the heart,
which receives the deadly weapon "to the feather."*

The Indian was by no means shy about eating a horse if he had
to; but astride one he had, almost magically, grown his own four
hooves to match the other flying hooves of the tall prairie grass.
Maybe there was never a hunter more glorious-looking than this
centaur of the Plains.

In his boyhood an Indian hunter would have been given toy
weapons to play with so he might familiarize himself with them. As
he grew, he would be shown how to find and kill small game,
graduating to big game in his youth. With his first kill of a large
animal he would be permitted to taste not one bite of the meat but
would have to give it all to his family and receive only his people's
praises in its stead. Not until he had demonstrated himself to be a
competent hunter—the quintessential "good provider"—would he
be considered fit to take a wife.

At the same time he learned the ways of animals, he was also
made aware of the respect due them. For the Indian, no line existed
dividing the material from the spiritual world. If a hunter showed
disrespect for the game he killed by purposely wasting the meat or
by not observing the proper rituals and taboos before and after the
hunt, then the spirit of the dead animal would send word to the
live-animal spirits and they would no longer permit this hunter to
kill their bodies. Besides these spirits there were other beings, such
as the half-man, half-animal Keeper of the Game or the Dwarfs of
the eastern forests, who could also punish a bad hunter—or reward a
good one.

The Indian hunter, therefore, felt that a compact of mutual
respect existed between him and the game he pursued; as long as he

treated the animal honorably, the animal would reciprocate by allowing its body to be killed and its flesh to be eaten over and over again, and the Indian would not starve. It was not purely fear or scruples that motivated the Indian to such a regard for game, however, but a genuine belief that game was *worthy* of his respect. After all, the Indian believed he was directly descended from the animal world, from the raven or the bear or the beaver or some other wild creature; animals, put simply, were people, his *own* people. (An Eskimo killing a whale, for example, might have to go into mourning for it as if it had been his own relative.) Did this, then, make the Indian hunter the tearstained saint in feathers and buckskin that became his popular image during "Ecology's" early halcyon days? Hardly. The Indian hunter was probably something a lot closer to a mystical pragmatist when it came to his treatment of game. He was no savior of animals; he was only a man of honor toward them.

Of course, the American Indian as a race of hunters living entirely off the land is as defunct today as Buffalo Bill. That has been seen to by history. And the very few "primitive" hunters still managing to walk the earth's face, such as the Yanomáma tribe of Amazonia or the !Kung Bushmen of the Kalahari, do so with an ever more tenuous step, war and development and disease and the rest of the hounds in "Progress's" pack ready to run them to ground at the first opportunity. Feeling people with hearts as big as all outdoors who would go to the mat for a seal pup—and will be sure to tell you so—seem in general to know very little and to care even less about the plight of such hunting peoples. Yet when we lose the last members of our species who dwell totally within nature—near-naked humans slipping silently from tree to tree through a rain forest somewhere, handmade arrows nocked to bowstrings of sinew—I dare say we shall all have lost something quite as invaluable as any extinguished breed of game.

Ishi the hunter, taken from his wild home of lava rock, Digger pines, salmon streams, and game trails, lived but a few years among the White Men. With no resistance to even a cold, he was continually stricken with illness. His brief time in civilization, however, does not seem to have been a truly unhappy one for him.

He was able to demonstrate to fascinated city dwellers many of the crafts a hunter needed to know in order to survive on his own, to tell the scientists about his life before he came to the slaughterhouse, to let his black hair grow long once more, to sing his songs and dance his dances. Once he was even able to return to his home with his white friends and hunt again, wearing only his breechclout and bathing for a final time in the icy flowing waters of the Yahi nation. Yet when the end came for him, Ishi, once a slayer of the elk and the bear, had become the only thing the world seemed to have any room for him to become: a relict. He died in a bed set up in an empty exhibit hall in the museum, the long hunt long over.

Northbound

For the first cartographers to lay eyes on it, that trackless north country must have seemed a land they could never hope to chart. Not until 1907, in fact, was the first reliable map of the northern interior of British Columbia published—the crowning achievement of the Oblate missionary Father A. G. Morice. (This priest managed—during the course of parochial and exploratory treks through the 70,000-square-mile expanse of wilderness that was his parish— to take the first accurate measure of the land, using only a compass, a chronometer, an aneroid barometer, a sounding line, and the oral reports of Carrier Indian hunters and guides.) Even today—though it is hatched with dirt roads cut through by government bureaucracies, timber companies, mining corporations, and various small-time laissez-faire-capitalist enterprises—the interior north of where the maintained dirt road ends in the outpost of Manson Creek (itself four hours north of where the tarmac plays out in the village of Fort St. James) appears in road atlases as so much *terra incognita.*

There are times of the year, however, when only *terra incognita* will do. In the fall I always seem to want to go lay eyes on such "unknown land." It might be some seasonal change in body chemistry that makes me nomadic, or maybe it is that the weather is cool and still dry and just right for traveling. Maybe it's just a good time to "get away." For whatever reason, in the fall I needed remote northern country to go into, and so I chose the Omineca Mountains, across the Pacific-Arctic Divide, to go hunt grouse in. Ruffed, Franklin's, and blue grouse, and willow and white-tailed ptarmigan—an entire assortment of Tetraonidae—make their homes in that country, yet grouse seem to have been, in all the rich history of the northern interior, among the least of reasons for venturing into its fastness.

It was beaver, whose pelts could be stretched into circles flat as drumheads and bundled off east to be made into felt hats to grace the heads of fashionable gentlemen, that brought the likes of Alexander Mackenzie and Simon Fraser (no less intrepid explorers by being equally intrepid merchants) into the interior—as beaver brought so many other like men to the Mountain West of all North America. Mackenzie and Fraser's North-West Fur-Trading Company's *engagés* were the first Europeans into British Columbia's northern interior, the first to erect trading posts in it, and the first to give it an English name other than "Unexplored"—the Scots Fraser calling it, after his homeland, New Caledonia. The North-West Company in time combined with the ubiquitous Hudson's Bay Company, and by 1836 the amalgamation was such a going concern in the area that, according to Father Morice's detailed accounting in *The History of Northern Interior British Columbia (Formerly New Caledonia),* "67,510 salmon; 11,941 of the smaller fish, plus 781 sturgeon and 346 trout; 2,160 rabbits; 153 ducks, 10 lynxes, 8 marmots, 3 porcupines, 1 swan . . . and 14 dogs" were used as provisions for the many employees of the numerous trading posts in a single twelvemonth—not counting, of course, an unrecorded number of horses that were also eaten.

In 1855 gold became another reason for venturing north into the interior, and it remains one today, with some people coming in with full-scale mining operations, and others with just the fever and a grubstake (and sometimes with just the fever), even though almost every worthwhile claim was staked long ago. They still come north to trap for furs, too, but also now to log and to guide and to hunt moose and caribou and mountain goat and wolf and black bear and grizzly. And not a few come for the naïve reason why many people have always headed into the northern wilderness to live—the notion that somehow, by going as far north as they can get, they will outdistance whatever was driving them loco "down there": an idea not without a certain appeal to many of us. But all too often, by the first January their cabin is only half built, the kids are croupy, the chain saw has cashed it in, and whatever was driving them crazy down there must have hidden under a tarp in the back of the '68 pickup and hitched along.

Which is why I intended to be in this north country for only a few days in the fall simply to hunt grouse. To live successfully in the North, you need a firm purpose to your being there—not merely some vague quest for wholeness—or the North can become crazier than any place you could have left behind: that country cracks greenhorns as though they were bargain china. But even without a firm purpose, if you go for only a short visit, and pick your spot well, it can still work magic. Bearing that in mind, I wrote to several guides in the northern interior, asking them what they knew about grouse. One replied.

Larry Erickson got my letter in late August while he was hurrying to finish the setting up of his spike camps in time for the season's hunts in the Cariboo Range. Someone's wanting to come north strictly for grouse hunting seemed a bit unusual to him at first; but, scratching his balding head under his green cap, he noticed that the return address was California, and that seemed to explain it—as it seems to explain so many other strange phenomena these days.

Taking time out from raising tents and trailing up pack animals, he sat down and wrote in blue ink beneath a letterhead with a mountain on it: "I have hunted Grouse myself & guided for

them, usually with Big Game, for over 25 years. I am a naturalist &
an avid bird watcher. I have trapped & lived in the Back Country
since early manhood."

Warming to the letter writing, he went on to explain to me, in
that headlong prose peculiar to outdoorsmen, the natural history of
grouse:

*Both Grouse & Ptarmigan populations are influenced by weather. Adult birds
require a high level of Protein in their diets to lay eggs & in turn the young
must have high Protein to survive. It takes hot summers with high air
temperatures to produce the Insect life needed to create & maintain a high
native Grouse & Ptarmigan population. It seems very possible that the high in
the Sun-Spot Cycle & the Grouse Cycle could be one in the same. The Snowshoe
Hare Cycle is another which may follow the Sun-Spot Cycle.*

*Ruffed Grouse in this Area are found at the lower levels in or near
Poplar (Aspen) stands. They have a Grey & Red phase. Both are common.
The meat is light, even in Adult birds.*

*Franklin's Grouse are usually found higher, mostly in or around Pine
stands. They have darker meat than that of the Ruffed Grouse, but are also
very good eating.*

*Blues are found near timberline in open Draws in the Balsam fir
(Alpine fir). Meat on young birds is light; but on old ones, especially old
males, it is dark & strong. At this time they are not plentiful up here. In
winter Ruffs eat willow & poplar buds, Franklins eat pine needles & Blues fir
needles.*

*White-tailed Ptarmigan are found above timberline on Rough Rocky
Mountains. They never get into big flocks like Willows. They drop down to
lower valleys in Early winter, usually in small Groups or Singles, unlike the
Willows who also come down in winter, but in big flocks.*

*Willow Ptarmigan are found in Open Mountain Valleys & in Moun-
tains that are rolling & gentle. At times in the Cycle they get into flocks of 2–
3 hundred. In the late fall the males cackle at dawn & are an excellent Alarm
Clock.*

If you, far south in some city, had awakened that morning to
the white noise coming from a clock radio, this was the kind of
letter that could make your day. I wrote back to Erickson, telling
him to expect me up in the northern interior of British Columbia in
mid-October, when I would do some grouse hunting.

I have noticed that a fault too many Westerners (American and Canadian alike) share is their low esteem for the intelligence of grouse. "Fool hens" is what they call them, and belittlingly describe ways to catch them with hand loops, or tell of how they shot an entire flock, one by one, out of the branches of a pine with a small-caliber rifle—how one season they killed and then canned scores and scores of them, those silly birds were that simple to knock off. What is never brought up, however, is how long into the season it was possible to wreak such havoc, or how far ahead of the hunter the birds started rising up after a while, or how deep in *terra incognita* these birds were found. What is hardly ever brought up is that the grouse is a bona fide wilderness dweller who, like the caribou, the grizzly, and the mountain sheep, cannot long tolerate men.

When, in mid-October, I came north to Fort St. James—with the old log buildings of the Hudson's Bay trading post still on the shore of Stuart Lake, and with the low quiet voices of Indians in the neon cafés—I found that the Western opinion of grouse was little different there. My guess would be that only a small minority of the grouse killed in the northern interior are taken with shotguns. The vast majority are killed incidental to big-game hunts or by passing motorists brandishing .22s out truck windows at the sight of the birds picking up grit along the road shoulders. The grouse are so famous for being attracted to the warm open spaces the roads provide for them in the dense timber, in fact, that when I told a resident of the "Fort" I was northbound to hunt birds, he enthusiastically told me that the drive up would offer excellent opportunity for sport. As it turned out, while his appraisal might have been accurate for the opening day of the season, it had nothing to do with the conditions to be found in mid-October: even if one were up for a little road hunting, by mid-October the grouse along the shoulders had been shot at (quite illegally) by about every timber faller and drill operator who passed by, and were as jittery and flighty as quail. These birds would have to be *hunted*.

From the Fort, then, I rode farther north in the weekly mail truck to Manson Creek—the neo-sourdough at the wheel telling me that he had downed his moose the Sunday before last, about a mile back into the woods behind his house, and was able to return for it, driving a skip loader from the lumber mill, and carry it out whole. Larry Erickson met me in Manson, and as we drove even farther north into the back country to his cabin, he revealed himself to be a man who had known from his boyhood that the only thing that would satisfy him in this world was to be a hunter and fur trapper in the wilds of British Columbia, and who in his "early manhood" left the prairies of Alberta behind, to buy a trapline around Germansen Lake in the Omineca Mountains. He still remembered, with some nostalgia, his first two winters up here when he had not seen another human until the thaw. Now he could say, with a twinge of bitterness, that he had neighbors within fifteen miles of him, year-round.

It had been snowing when we left Manson—Erickson saying that of all the country around in any direction, including north, winter came to these mountains first, and did not leave until weeks after spring had come everywhere else. (But with this sunspot cycle, he added, the weather seemed to be changing every which way, with the winters turning warmer and wetter and the animal herds ebbing and flowing all over one another's ranges.) Now, however, as we drove along the shore of Germansen Lake, the sky was blue and untouched. We stopped once to saw up a poplar a beaver had felled across the road, and after three hours of driving from Manson we turned off onto a dirt road of twin ruts, running across a frozen meadow and climbed up to log corrals and cabins set at the foot of a mountain—Erickson quick to point out to me, as we pulled up and stopped, a northern shrike chasing a hapless whisky jack into the pines.

A set of moose antlers was nailed to the roof over the porch of Erickson's cabin. Around the cabin and back into the woods were scattered the low houses to which his pure-blooded Eskimo sled dogs were tethered. Their bloodcurdling howls echoed through the trees as we got out of the truck, but once you let these hundred-pound animals off their chains and into the cabin, they would try to climb into your lap and lick your face. Erickson said they were the only means of transportation he had in the winter to get him around his trapline; and when he was out on the trail at sixty below, he would bed down at night with bull caribou hides wrapped around his sleeping bag, and with his dog team huddled around him—

sleeping as snug as a bug until all the animals erupted in a snarling dogfight at the stroke of midnight.

After supper, Erickson led me down to my cabin, telling me not to be concerned about the possibility of a young local grizzly nosing around the place at night, then wished me a good night's rest. Inside my cabin I lit the lamp and wondered what I would do without country like this—populated by trappers and sled dogs; where even a nighttime visit to the privy could have the makings of a bear story—to get away to every so often. Not that I believed I was far enough north yet to be kept from *ever* going loco, but at least I was far enough north now to keep—for a while longer anyway— from becoming even more a part of the strange phenomena of these days than I already was. Holding that thought, I cupped my hand around the lamp chimney and blew out the light.

The Franklin's were in the pines below in the morning. As I carried my shotgun through the spongy wet dimness in the trees, Erickson beside me said that sometimes all that had to be done in hunting Franklin's was to stand still in the forest and the Franklin's would begin calling out, announcing their whereabouts to you. Today, though, the birds burst out of the branches near the tops of the trees with no cries at all. Killing a male, I hefted him in my hand, seeing the inky darkness of his feathers, the white spotting on his breast, the fierce redness of the comb above his eye. Fool hen, indeed. We hunted on.

The ruffed grouse, Roger Tory Peterson writes, is "usually not seen until it springs into the air with a startling whir." As we hunted ruffs through the long shadows slanting over the leaves on the ground in a poplar grove that afternoon, I saw his point. We jumped them out of what seemed no cover whatsoever, then followed them deeper into the grove, rising them up again and again as I shot and Erickson gathered up the downed birds. He told me that in winter these birds would dive beneath the snow at night for insulation, and in the morning they were always exploding into the air from beneath your snowshoes as you traversed the country. Wolves were quite partial to grouse, he said, and once he had witnessed a big silver wolf leaping ten feet into the air to catch a grouse on the wing, like a dog jumping for a treat.

In the northern interior of British Columbia, the sun never finds its way much above the level of the treetops, and by two-thirty in the afternoon in mid-October the light has gone golden in the sky. Erickson and I had some traveling to do to be back in camp by dark, so we packed up the birds and headed in. At twilight in his camp, Erickson cleaned the birds, showing me the highbush cranberries, clover, and rose hips in the crops of the ruffs, the bundles of pine needles in the crops of the Franklin's. He would tack the wings out on boards to dry, then use them as lynx flags over his trap sets, where the dangling wings would catch the eye of furbearers.

We ate mountain goat steaks for dinner that night, and with our hot coffee in the gray morning had mountain goat liver. Then, saddling two horses—mine a 1,200-pound gelding named Bucky— we rode up the mountain to find ptarmigan and the winter.

Down at Erickson's cabin a light rain fell, dripping from the moose antlers; but as we climbed, the rain turned to snow piling up in heavy "whisky-jack blankets" on the bent fir branches. On the trail, though, we could still mark the signs of pine marten, weasel, rabbit, wolf, and a track Erickson was unfamiliar with, but which I took to be the biggest mule deer track I had ever seen. He thought it was a bit far afield for mule deer, but said that, with the weather change, he wouldn't question it.

After climbing two thousand feet on horseback, we crossed the timberline and came out in rolling draws where moose had cropped down the willow bush as flat-topped as ornamental shrubbery. Ahead of us in the bush bobbed the black-eyed heads of a flock of willow ptarmigan, whiter than the snow around them now that all their summer plumage was gone. Swinging off Bucky, I drew my 12-gauge from the scabbard and loaded it. Erickson held the horses' reins while I crept toward the birds. When I got up on them, seven black-tailed birds flushed, fanning out like the back of a stud-poker hand. After I emptied both barrels, two bright birds lay on the fresh snow, making it look dingy in comparison. I carried the birds back to Erickson, and he told me his last story, that while he had once seen a wolf catch a ruff, another time he had seen one of these white birds outfly a peregrine falcon in full pursuit of it.

" 'Old Haggle-Bird of the North,' they're called," Erickson said—for their incessant cackling. He carefully put the birds I gave him into his day pack.

Tethering the horses, we had to climb higher on foot, to the broken rock up on the mountainside, before we found any white-tailed ptarmigan—slightly smaller than the willows. The snow, collected in the shallow gulches, crested above our knees, so we used the long grass poking above it to locate the ridges we could travel on more easily. Nearly at the crest, with the sun weak on it, we found the whitetails perched fat and round on bare snow. They flushed in front of us and I fired. While I removed the empty shells from my gun, a bird died with his white wings outspread as if in an embrace of the snow. After a while we rode down off the mountain.

For dinner that night we ate grouse—the meat of the ruffs as fine as that of any pheasant, and the Franklin's and ptarmigan's wild and dark. Afterward I said good night to Erickson and, untroubled by the prospect of bear, walked out across the brittle snow, past the shapes of dogs sleeping and horses shifting from hoof to hoof in the corrals. In the cabin I lit the lamp again and adjusted the wick so it would not smoke. Then I built the biggest fire I could fit into the Favorite Box 25 stove and hung my damp socks and jacket around it and sat staring into its open door. When the fire had burned all the way down, I got into my sleeping bag and blew out the lamp.

In the darkness I could feel the cold seep back into the cabin. I tried to remember everything, exactly, so I could carry it intact with me when I headed back "down there" in the morning. There were Erickson's stories and the walking and the riding and the Franklin's and the ruffs and the willows and the whitetails all flaring up out of my memory. But no blues. At this time they are not plentiful up here. There must be some out there, though, where no one is able to find them in this remote northern country I do not know what I should do without.

I thought about that as I lay in my sack of feathers with my head to the north, to the Arctic Sea where the rivers flowed and where, beyond maps, the light of the aurora came down upon the pole in red and yellow and blue and . . .

Elk in the Highwood

Elk, what do you eat?
Sage I eat.
Elk, what dish do you use?
Stone dish I do use.
            —ANCIENT BLACKFOOT CHILDREN'S SONG

The real charm of an elk is, in truth, that he will eat about whatever's set in front of him, stone dish or no. His balanced diet is drawn from a most catholic list of foods, from buttercups to clover to pines to mushrooms, with a bull eating his own shed antler velvet or a cow consuming her placenta to conceal all trace of her calf's birth. An elk *will* even eat sage.

This utter lack of finicalness always served the elk well, particularly during that time when he was the most far-flung of American deer—indeed, of American ungulates. He was once, outside of such extremities as Maine and Florida, a native of almost any place on the continent between the Atlantic and Pacific littorals and from the Subarctic well down into Mexico. Ten million is the figure often quoted for the elk's peak population in this expanse of land, prior to our seizing of beachheads in the wake of Columbus' monumental wade ashore.

When the early colonists of New England encountered two new varieties of deer, they quickly named one, the whitetail, "deer" after their island home's roe deer. Nothing in their past experience, however, had prepared them for the sight of the other, the one the Shawnee called *wapiti,* meaning "white rump," which was so large and unfamiliar a beast to them that they resolved to call it *elk,* concluding it must be quite similar to the European moose of the same name—a beast with which they also happened to be completely unfamiliar. But no matter, the Pilgrim Fathers *did* learn in short order that this elk was exceptional fare; and that 10 million figure, if ever correct, did not remain so for long. By 1922 the number was more like 90,000 for the entire continent. Only after long struggle and much good effort has the species been restored today to a strong half-million head in North America.

When, in 1755 in the company of Crees, the fur trader Anthony Henday became the first white man to venture into the Blackfoot country of Alberta (then part of that vast stretch of Canadian soil known as Rupert's Land, which comprised all the drainage of Hudson Bay and in 1670 had been granted by the English monarch to the Hudson's Bay Company), he would observe elk roaming all across its southern plains, the animal (both Rocky Mountain and Manitoban subspecies) being distributed at that time throughout the province's present geographical area to within fifty miles of the Northwest Territories' southern boundary. Then during the nineteenth century the great extirpation, by many causes but mostly by the hand of man, got under way. Before it ended, all of Alberta could boast in 1913 of having exactly as many elk as the days in a

year. (Even at that, however, the elk of Alberta were still doing far
better than the Eastern and the Merriam subspecies, which had
already been handed their hats and shown to the Big Door.)

Before the period between 1917 and 1920 when Rocky Mountain elk, transplanted from Yellowstone—the great incubator and
salvation of the species—would be reintroduced into Alberta and
eventually bring about a regeneration to the current 19,000 or so
animals, the province's wapiti herds shrank to at most three, of
which one, totaling only a score or so elk, retreated to this
Highwood Range here in the foothills of Alberta's Rockies
southwest of Calgary. It may be that the herd had even retreated as
far back as 9,126-foot Mount Head there in the dark western sky,
the mountain rising like a granite cake made of a dozen thin layers
filled in between with white icing.

The mountain swallowed our western horizon. From the bare
hill we had climbed before dawn on this cold Tuesday morning in
late October, the Austrian-born Alberta Registered Class A Guide,
my friend Paul, and I took turns using the guide's Austrian spotting
telescope to look north across the valley of Sullivan Creek at the herd
of elk feeding distantly up a draw of yellow timothy grass pasture.
As the sun slid into the valley, we could distinguish the bulls'
antlers at that far reach, not as solid acorn-colored branches, but as
faint nimbi of ivory tips carried high above their heads. These elk
were not going to remain in the open for long in the daylight,
though; and as we watched, in single file they all moved into the
spruce and poplars standing around the pasture's edge and were
gone. The guide collapsed his telescope between his hands, and we
headed down off the hill. Elk season opened the next day.

On the day before this, though, Paul and I had already gone
with the guide onto the prairies south of the gas town of Brooks and
watched the guide in his knickers and knee socks—the young
Austrian a certifiable walking fool—speed across the broken land on
foot. As I watched through my binoculars from a distance of a
quarter-mile, the morning air chill and clear as a piece of Baccarat
crystal, I saw the guide run the last few yards to a low rise in the
sage and flop onto his stomach. In front of him ranged a milling

herd of pronghorn, each animal's hide portioned out in bands of white and tawny and black. The guide laid the cross hairs of his .25-'06 Steyr on the biggest buck.

I saw the buck flinch terminally before I ever heard the shot. As the rest of the herd fled, the big dying antelope ran after them, going in great lunging staggers until he pitched down and was still, the 115-grain bullet having passed through the lobes of both lungs. That was the opening morning of Alberta's pronghorn season, and after field-dressing the antelope, we loaded him into the back of the guide's friend's pickup to carry him back to the friend's ranch to skin him. As we were pulling into the yard, however, the rancher spotted dark, nearly black, pheasant cocks running into a brake of leafless willows on the edge of a cut wheat field, and I got to watch again as the guide took out his 12-gauge and in five minutes returned with his limit of three birds. That was as much *watching* as I could stand, and that afternoon I bought my nonresident alien's elk license.

Back in Calgary that Monday night, Paul and I ate hot moose sausages and potato salad with the guide and his wife in their home before going out to the garage with him to pluck the pheasants.

As we stood around pulling the feathers off the scalded and drawn birds, the guide told us how he had come to Alberta from hotel and restaurant school in Austria with no funds and only a job in a hotel waiting for him. In his kitchen, after we had finished with the pheasants and he was deftly butchering up the antelope, summarily turning it into butterflied steaks, roasts, schnitzel, and stew meat ("You must use meat with *sinew* for stews," he instructed, trimming an antelope shank down to the pale yellow bone. "A stew is never good the first time you cook it, but only after it has been *re*heated two or three times. Without sinew, you end up with a . . . a . . . *meat soup!*"), the guide told us how he had gone from kitchen worker to being a sommelier to managing restaurants to at last becoming an owner in one of Calgary's finest French restaurants. In Alberta he had also found the kind of hunting he always longed for when he lived as a boy in Europe and some of his greatest sport had been poaching the trout from the parish priest's private beat. He would confess this crime to the priest himself every Sunday morning before serving Mass for him, only to have to slink back into the confessional again the next Sunday morning, the very same sin once more blackening his immortal soul and causing him to tremble with an almost lustful delight. Within days of his arrival in the New World he had gone out on his own and taken his first royal elk, this leading him inevitably into guiding.

It was the immigrant's story. Later, over delicate and finely made pewter tumblers of ten-year-old schnapps, the guide brought out the photo album and showed us the family castle.

The next morning, after coming down off that hill after scouting the elk, we drove into the creek valley on a gravel road and came to the guide's other friend Laurie's T-L Ranch, out of which we would be hunting. Laurie, wearing his red rancher's cap and a beaded and fringed elk-hide jacket, greeted us in his faint voice that made him sound as though he were forever sharing a confidence. He was skinny but strong and walked in the slightly creaky way of someone who in his younger days had climbed up on 'em and let 'em buck, which he had. In his way he was as much an immigrant to this land as the guide, his family having broken and settled it just a generation before. Besides being the edge of the elk's original range in Alberta, this Highwood country had not so long ago been the edge of the Blackfoot's home territory as well.

The Blackfoot was a Plains Indian, but his vision quests might often bear him up to such high hazardous places as Mount Head back there, where he would build his tiny lodge of brush and leaves and for many days, through singing and prayer and fasting and dreams, would wait alone for his own spirit helper to come to him to show him the way for his life to follow. Beside him he would keep his filled pipe, ready to offer it to his secret helper when he came. And often he came in the shape of Elk.

Although nomads of the plains, which they burned down with some regularity—and in so doing maintained the grasslands and benefited the wild grazers—and people of the buffalo, which they ran down on the prairies or drove over cliffs such as Old Woman's Buffalo Jump near Cayley, just a little ways east of the T-L Ranch, the Blackfoot were also chronic hunters of the elk, which they insisted—unlike other tribes who feared the big deer's turning and goring them and their riding stock—upon pursuing entirely from horseback. Actually, the Blackfoot insisted upon pursuing *everything* from horseback, feeling—like the Northern Shoshoni and the mountain men who learned their etiquette from them—demeaned if called upon to cover even the least distance on foot. (James Willard Schultz, another fur trader and a hunting guide of the late 1800s, could write of his adopted Blackfoot tribe's "slender-legged men who hunted on horseback or not at all," and not fear contradiction.)

Perhaps the Blackfoot sat so resolutely astride his pony because he recalled with little nostalgia the time before that animal's appearance on the scene when he had been a dog Indian, his mobility limited by how heavy a pack load his meat-eating dog could carry, or how big a travois it could drag. When at last he got the horse, the Blackfoot took a careful measurement of it against the dog and wondered how he had ever managed to live so long without his trusty steed. As for the dog, the Blackfoot's years of forced familiarity with it had probably bred such fierce contempt that this was the reason the tribe, unlike neighboring ones who found it quite the delicacy, steadfastly refused ever to dine upon the creature.

It was from horseback, then, and at any season, that the prideful Blackfoot overtook the elk on the prairies or rode it over jumps or drove it into water where he could kill it with his bow or lance or Winchester '73. He found a lone animal more difficult to catch, more prone to running on, while it was usually easier to cut one out of a herd as the animals bumped and ran into each other, tiring themselves out more rapidly. The Blackfoot's preference was for a large mature bull who would yield the most meat. The effort required for taking a smaller animal was not that much less, while the rewards could be considerably so. It was simple economics, yet the Blackfoot also taught his sons to take the bull elk for their exemplar of gallantry.

Though the buffalo were the main source of the Blackfoot's not inconsequential wealth—permitting him, when the herds were more like a broad phenomenon of the local climate, like average days of sunshine or annual rainfall, than a collection of individual organisms, a life of some luxury marked by regular feasting and gambling—the elk were also of great value to him. Curiously, he was not overly fond of the flavor of elk meat, finding it too "sweet," too much like the white man's prized beef, yet he would turn to it readily enough whenever he could not obtain bison. (All parts of the elk were eaten by the Blackfoot, noted George Bird Grinnell, the great hyphenate who in his lifetime was an anthropologist-conservationist-sportsman-explorer-author and member of any number of other chosen professions—"save only the lungs, gall, and one or two other organs.")

From the elk hide the Blackfoot made robes, shirts, dresses, dancing skirts, moccasins, leggings, war shields; some tipis, lean-tos, and ground cloths; parfleches, ropes, and belts. He would use it also as an item of exchange in intertribal bartering. The antlers served him as bows, as we know, and as saddletrees and fleshing tools, the points becoming wedges for splitting wood or for the knapping of his flint arrowheads before he turned to iron to tip his shafts. As many as the products and trophies from the elk were, though, the ones most esteemed were its tusks.

These two round upper canines, stained by plant juices, called bugler teeth, whistlers, or simply ivories, had been used as ornamentation by the Indian for almost fifty centuries. No other part of any animal, not bear teeth and claws, not the fangs and claws of cougars, not wolf teeth, bison teeth, or even *horse* teeth, was so highly valued. They were the Indian's "Star of Delhi."

It was the immense effort that went into gaining the ivories that gave them such worth. Years of hunting and bargaining with other hunters were needed to acquire the sometimes hundreds, or in one case over 1,500, elk teeth required to sequin a squaw's dress. A dying hunter would bequeath his ivories to his heirs as their legacy. The Crow, instead of having to quest for their visions and "medicine," might purchase them outright for the sum of 500 ivories—though who the merchant could be for such a transaction I cannot say. One tremendously wealthy Shoshoni village in southern Montana, visited by a Chicago newspaper writer in 1901, was reported to have 20,000 ivories in its possession. Though the Blackfoot came to value the elk's ivories only about the time he obtained firearms, a woman's gown adorned with only a single horizontal row of teeth might fetch in trade two good horses, each "the best buffalo horse."

The white man, to be sure, was not insensible to the worth of the elk either. Theodore Roosevelt, only indulging in the barest of hyperbole, declared it "the largest and stateliest deer in the world." Other white men, market hunters, saw to it in the 1850s that the restaurants of San Francisco, always the center of fine dining—as well as the restaurants of other cities—would not be without fresh elk steaks to offer on their daily menus. The hide hunters—only one cut in the Indian's and the general public's estimations above the wolfers who plied their trade by first shooting down a buffalo, liberally lacing the carcass with strychnine, then paying periodic visits to it to skin out the numerous dead wolves scattered about the area in postures of frozen anguish—rode into Blackfoot country on the crest of the buffalo-hunting wave; but when that particular tide receded they stayed on to look after the elk.

In 1874 young George Bird Grinnell, wearing his naturalist's hat, was given that official position with George Armstrong Custer's Black Hills Expedition—an expedition to which Custer, that grand fanfaron of the Great Plains, saw that a full regimental band mounted on white horses, to play the men out in the morning and perform concerts at night, was attached. Grinnell's work for Custer apparently came to the attention of Captain William Ludlow, who asked the Yale graduate to join him the next year on an exploration of Yellowstone, lately made the world's first national park.

The spectacle Yellowstone presented to Grinnell, however, was not enough to blind him to what he saw on his passage through Montana and Wyoming. The hide hunters were out there in full force, and Grinnell felt compelled to report to Ludlow on the "terrible destruction of large game" that he witnessed. "It is estimated," he wrote, "that during the winter of 1874–75 not less than 3,000 elk were killed for their hides alone." As late as 1881, five thousand hide hunters were still hard at work in southern Canada, the Dakotas, Montana, and Wyoming. Sometimes they did not even bother with the hide, but killed an elk solely for the two ivories.

It is tempting, naturally, to assume that the Blackfoot and

other Indians might have been wise enough to stay well clear of such a tragedy, but at a time when the nation's per capita income stood at a good bit less than $200.00 per annum, and a green elk hide would bring $7.00, it would be plain quixotry to believe there was any way they could. When the buffalo had gone, so had the Plains Indians' subsistence way of life, and they found themselves needing the white man's tobacco, his kettles, his blankets, his alcohol. So they killed more animals more wastefully.

Before the 1870s a brave acquired elk ivories only to present them to his squaw, choosing for himself to wear no more than one or two on a pendant or a bracelet. (The only men who did wear elk ivories on their clothes were homosexual transvestites—who were nonetheless held in high regard by their tribes—or "clowns" who impersonated women on ceremonial occasions.) But as the Indian encountered increasing numbers of white men—many of whom who had probably never even seen an elk, let alone hunted one—all wearing with much self-satisfaction the ivories of elk on the fobs dangling out of the watch pockets of their vests, he, too, began in sad mimicry to don his own ivoried vest.

At the conclusion of his epoch as a hunter of the elk, the Indian could be found outside his lodge, carving from bone simulacra of ivories to sell to white men. The workmanship was said to be first-rate, and to the untrained eye the final product was nearly indistinguishable from the genuine article.

That was all some time ago, of course. And the amazing thing of it is not what the elk was subjected to, but that he survived it, and with the eventual aid of sounder laws and sounder management—in short, greater restrictions on men's hands—survived it so well; so well, in fact, that we are still able to hunt him today.

On opening morning of Alberta's Big Game Zone 11 General Male Elk Season on the T-L Ranch, then, the guide and Paul are gone long before dawn, climbing swiftly—the only speed the Austrian knows—on foot through the darkness up the backside of the ridge above the timothy grass pasture, packing their rifles and binoculars and the spotting telescope. Laurie and I are going to ride—across another adjacent pasture, then into the timber and far back into the country we believe the elk will be passing through later as the sun rises.

The coffee is still warm in me as I come out of the old cabin where I slept in a bed with an old white-painted stead of iron, carrying across the ranch yard my beeswaxed rifle scabbard over one arm and my .375 slung on my shoulder. Beyond the log rails of the corral fence I see the square block of light inside the stable where Laurie is saddling our horses. Looking up, I can see in the night sky the bright fires of all the constellations whose names I still have not gotten around to knowing.

The horse Laurie is saddling for me is part thoroughbred and part quarter horse. He is a big gray gelding (a color that does not exist, since it is really a mix of white and black hairs) who in the daylight looks almost blue. His name is Joker, and Joker is a mite wild.

As best as I can gather it from what Laurie seems to be whispering to me in the stable, up until this past moose season when he and the guide had used Joker as a pack animal, the horse had been as solid as Gibraltar. Then came an unbalanced load, a smashed pannier, and about four hundred pounds of dead moose scattered to hell and gone again across a willow swamp, and Joker was left a little on the touchy side. As we wait for some light to come into the eastern sky before setting out, I spend my time stroking Joker's head and neck and shamelessly trying to ingratiate myself into his good graces.

The weather, Laurie tells me while we wait, is not good. Too dry and warm for this time of year. Too likely to keep the elk in the timber where stalking up on them will be very difficult. This opening morning will give us the best chance for taking an elk until the snows finally come later in the season and push the herds down.

At last in gray light (which may also not exist) we saddle up and ride out the corral gate and across Sullivan Creek, named for a family of dead pioneer children who were taken by disease. We ride up out of the creek bed and onto the edge of the pasture, and even with me hauling manfully on his reins, Joker sets sail directly into a pile of brush and dead timber. We tack and maneuver awhile and I manage to get him back in line with Laurie, who compliments me on my horsemanship. I smile at him modestly—though I will admit that in the dim light somebody could easily have taken it for the rictus of sheer terror.

We are riding silently through Herefords in the large pasture, heading for that timber at the far end, when Laurie pulls up his horse and stares across to a distant edge of the pasture.

"Elk," he whispers, even more softly than usual.

There is still not enough light for me to recognize them clearly, but Laurie gets down and uses his binoculars, then swings back into the saddle. We sweep wide and move out to the pasture's edge where it abuts the poplars and spruces growing down off a high east-facing ridge. We dismount and tether the horses to the trees, my heart exalted to be off Joker's back. Pulling my .375 from the scabbard, I follow Laurie.

"Hurry. Quiet. Hurry. Quiet," he alternately commands as we move through the trees. Then there is the herd in front of us, grazing on the pasture's edge fewer than two hundred yards away, behind them a lingering polyp of the spruce timber extending into the pasture, with more empty pasture beyond it sloping back down to Sullivan Creek. Laurie points out the bull. It is hard to calculate tines, but from the length and volume of his rack, and for my first elk, he looks more than respectable.

One of the cows begins to move up the slope into the trees, and I can see that their morning feeding is all but ended. This seems sooner in the hunt to kill an elk than it should be—certainly sooner than I had anticipated—but as in hunting any big-game animal, it is the elk who has set the agenda. So with great care and as much silence as I can achieve I work the bolt on my Model 70 and chamber a 270-grain round. Taking a rest on a stump, I let all the cow elk drift out from behind the nearly snowy bull, his belly and neck and raised head chocolaty in color, his antlers laid back. I let off the safety, draw in a breath and expel one half of it, put the reticle at the juncture of his neck and shoulder, and *sque-e-e-e-eze* the trigger. And miss. A classic clean All-American warning shot, known in every sporting country around the globe. No harm, though hardly no foul. As the elk all wheel and stampede down into the spruce peninsula behind them, I am tempted to shout after them, "Only kidding!" while dancing a little jig and waggling my hands like jackass ears at the sides of my head, the silver bells jingling merrily from the many peaks of my fool's cap.

Laurie, on the other hand, knowing exactly where the elk are headed, takes off at a dead run; I, behind him, at a dead trot. We wind along a game trail at the edge of the pasture, which carries us across the neck of the spruce stand. Then we can see the open pasture below, and there is the bull standing at the edge of it with two cows, the rest of the herd already gone into the trees and headed for the ridge crest. The bull is out a little over 320 paces in distance, and there is no place for me to take a rest. I sit, but the wild grass is too tall, so I have to kneel to see over it. I work the action once more, and the bull is standing broadside to me, and this time the sound I hear of the bullet hitting his shoulder is louder than the shot itself.

The bull turns away from the cows as they bolt into the trees and walks slowly out into the pasture. I run down to a young broken poplar and take a rest on its greenish, smooth bark. The distance is now 265 paces when I work the bolt and hit him again. He begins to stagger, his head down low to the ground, then he topples. We hurry down to him.

He is lying quietly with his head up, the cows barking to him from the timbered ridge. Another bull up there somewhere whistles. The hardiness and defiance of elk are legend—actually they *surpass* legend—and when we get to within 80 paces of him he recognizes us and leaps to his feet. Now he is a mass of energy, the E in him equaling something far in excess of mc^2 as he tries to escape. My final shot breaks his neck as he runs.

He lies within the perimeter of the stand of young poplars, the naked trees like a gray mist spreading down the ridge face. I jack out my empty cartridge and set my open rifle against a tree. In honor of the guide's Old World traditions, I cut a *Bruch* (branch) from the nearest tree and give the elk his "last bite." Clipping the metal license tag around the base of his antlers, I kneel and lift them up.

The antlers are long-pointed and ivoried. One side has five

points; the other, six. Each of the six points has a name. They are brow tine, bez tine (or bay tine or simply "dog killer," the tine the elk can sight along like a fencer sighting along his foil when it is carried *en garde,* and which should be longer than the brow tine), trez tine, dagger tine, and the forked terminal. Even the raised beaded rim around the seal where the antler base joins the pedicel has its name, being called the coronet. An elk bull has to grow an entirely new set of antlers, from coronets to terminals, every year.

This is how he grows them: triggered by testosterone and nerves, an antler buds out of the *pedicel* (part of the elk's forehead bone and the remnant of his ancient "dawn antler") by a buildup of cartilage, which under the blood-rich velvet covering creates a fibrous bone matrix that becomes impregnated with inorganic materials—mostly ash and calcium and phosphorus—mineralizing, in its way, not unlike the petrifying of a tree. The result after the velvet is shed is dead bone stained dark by the elk's slashing and rubbing against plants and trees, with the tips polished ivory white and the tines constructed along a six-point plane so the bulls can grapple with each other but still be able to disengage easily.

Yet as I sit beside my dead elk—the first dead elk of my life—waiting for Laurie to bring the horses down so we can dress and pack out the animal, watching still another herd of Albertan wapiti move over the top of the ridge, followed in only a minute or two by the skulking black shape of a cow moose traversing the sun-warmed face of the ridge—the moose all long white-stockinged legs and lumbering trepidation—I much prefer not to consider science but to wonder of these antlers how many fine hunting bows the Blackfoot could have made from them.

When I leave Alberta, I carry into Calgary's modern jet airport, built out on a stretch of prairie where the Blackfoot once ran their extravagant herds of horses, one fleshed elk skull and antlers, a fleshed and salted elk hide, a large quantity of cut and frozen and wrapped elk meat (including meat with sinew for stews), and two elk ivories tucked into the top left pocket of my buffalo-plaid shirt. At customs they ask me what it is I have to declare, and the answer seems obvious. Or not.

Kodiak

That journal I kept each day of my first hunt for Kodiak bear was a ledger of disappointment. Or so it seemed at the time. For fifteen days in the fall of 1978 I sat on the black gravel beaches of Kodiak Island, Alaska, in snow and sleet and downpour and gale, and glassed the white peaks above Uyak Bay—when they were visible—for sign of a good boar bear. Whenever I sighted one, though, he always seemed to be 4,000 feet high, moving through deep snow to the mountaintop to cross over and den up beyond reach on the other side. One particularly memorable day I watched a big boar—an animal weighing half a ton or better—quite literally swim through soft snow coming up to his chin. Reaching a tall, sheer face of naked rock, this bear reared and without pausing proceeded straight up like a fly on a windowpane. I lowered my binoculars in amazement and frustration and that night in camp wrote something uncalled for in my journal.

On a typical day of that hunt I might record sighting as many as nine bear, sows with cubs; how one set walked right by me on the beach with that deceptive ponderousness of theirs; or how the late Master Guide Park Munsey's head assistant (a Karluk man with the wonderful name of Bill Ambrosia) and I spent three hours in the alders and snow giving chase to a boar whose nonstop track showed that he had not had the common decency to break stride even once. And as you already know, after my fifteen-day brown bear permit expired, and having sighted nearly fifty bear without firing a shot, I went out on that sixteenth day with Bob Munsey and used my deer permit to take, as I wrote in what appeared to be the only bright spot in an otherwise dark journal, "a beautiful little blacktail buck among wild roses."

As can all too easily happen, though, when we look as hard as we can for one thing, we may overlook something else even more important. So it was not until one gray dawn in the last seemingly hopeless days of that hunt, as I was heading up the bay in an open Whaler, that I came unexpectedly to see that I had no choice but to return to Kodiak. And only many months later, when I could bring myself to read over my journal again, did I understand from the way I had written of it that the rare, stark beauty of that island had come to haunt me. To haunt me no more, however, than had its bear.

The haunted, out of a certain spiritual compulsion, seem to spend long nights; and late into those nights, often in some saloon at least twenty-five degrees south of the Forty-ninth State, some nouveau Klondiker down from the pipeline or off a trawler or just out of the air force, once he learns you, too, have seen Alaska, will try to tell you his "monster-killer-pointblank" Kodiak bear story. When the big brown bear has come to shamble through your head the way he shambles over green muskeg, such a tale will anger you at first, then only leave you saddened. "What a crock of vivid recollections!" you will feel like shouting at the end of it. But probably won't bother to.

At such a time, however, some things just have to be said about *Ursus arctos middendorffi,* the Kodiak bear, the "great grass-eating bear," the "great fish-eating bear," because, even though he is the world's largest land-going carnivore, none of his kind ever weighed a full ton or stood ten feet tall; and his reputation as a savage man-killer won't hold very much water. He is more than impressive enough without cheap exaggeration.

A truly big Kodiak bear, you should carefully and calmly point out, might weigh between 1,200 and 1,400 pounds, depending on the season; and his hide can *square* out at ten foot or so. His sense of smell will be nonpareil, his hearing keen, and he will be more or less blind as a Mexican free-tailed bat. In moments of inspiration he can cover ground like a track star or move all day at a pace no man could ever hope to match. And although the big brown bear has in him more curiosity than fear—and rogue bears have not been unheard of—he will be far and away more likely to steer a path around men than into them when he knows they are about.

No big-game animal besides him is native to the island, though various ones have been introduced. Every summer throughout the millennia the Kodiak has had to forage on spawning fish, and this protein-rich food is thought to have given his race its enormous size, and will add two hundred pounds or more to his weight between spring and fall. Some people have even gone so far as to suggest that because of his pleasant island diet of vegetation and salmon he may have a far milder disposition than his smaller cousin, as wonderfully named as Bill Ambrosia: *Ursus arctos horribilis,* the grizzly bear.

That *is* one way of looking at him, I suppose, but I do like to recall that he is of the very same biological genus as the fabled cave bear of the Pleistocene, *Ursus spelaeus,* and to look upon him as the last representative of the megafauna—American lions, dire wolves, saber-tooth tigers, giant bison and ground sloths, *mammoths!*—who onetime roamed the wide, snow-free plain of Beringia—created between northeastern Siberia and western Alaska when the last ice age lowered the sea level some 300 feet and uncovered the Bering Shelf. In any event, what has been termed the Kodiak bear's "brute power" is indeed awesome (Bill Ambrosia once saw a wounded boar bite clean through an alder branch big around as a baseball bat), and in the event of your wounding or cornering him, he would have no trouble making hash out of you in what is widely regarded as "a jiffy."

A Russian zoologist, Middendorf, you might go on to say, was the first scientist to report the huge bear of Kodiak Island, in a paper published in 1851. And in 1896 it fell to the American biologist Clinton Hart Merriam to present the first complete description of him. (Dr. Merriam was so thorough in his job, in fact, that he described eighty-six *distinct* species of brown and grizzly bear, based on the techniques of microscopic taxonomy then popular at Harvard University. It is believed today, however, that much the same blood flows in the veins of all the big brown bears of Asia, Europe, and North America, with what physical dissimilarities there may be among them arising from wide geographic separation and not the *fait accompli* of a difference in species.)

If you felt up to it, you could also tell of how, during the late nineteenth century—following a sudden downturn in the buffalo market—a lively trade in bear robes sprang up, and the big brown bear was liberally slaughtered along the Alaskan coast and on Kodiak Island in the enterprise. The robes taken from bear all over Alaska were shipped out through the port of Kodiak by the Alaska Commercial Company, so the name *Kodiak* was applied indiscriminately to all big brown bears, whether found on the mainland or on the island. Luckily for all big brown bears, this robe trade dried up with the amending in 1902 of the Alaska Civil Code to provide for the protection of *Ursus arctos,* if only rudimentarily. The bear came back after that, but within living memory some outdoor writers could still describe the elemental thrill of dropping a sow and her three yearling cubs in their tracks, or of taking *several* big boars on a single hunt; and as late as 1922 a Juneau newspaper would denounce a political hopeful merely by declaring a vote for him tantamount to a vote for the Alaskan brown bear, believed then to be worthy only of extinction because of his taste for salmon—the coastal dwellers' main cash crop. Today, any bear may still be taken under the overly vague justification of "in defense of life or property," but the licensed hunter is restricted to one adult bear, unaccompanied by cubs, every four years. Browns and grizzlies are grouped together in this, so anyone taking a big brown bear would have to wait four years before he could obtain a permit to hunt another brown *or* a grizzly, and vice versa. Frequently, the wife of a man somehow dissatisfied with the big brown bear he took on a hunt will develop a sudden unexplained interest in bear hunting within a year or less and put in for a tag herself. Her husband always seems to be good enough to accompany her on the hunt.

That Captain Charley Madsen was the very first bear guide on Kodiak Island you might not like to say for sure; but he was the first one everyone seems to recall. At least as early as the 1910s, this old-time trading-vessel skipper had taken up guiding for big brown bear on the peninsula and all over the island. Then came Hal Waugh, Alaska Master Guide No. One, who worked for Madsen before striking out on his own (and by following this lineage one can locate both Park Munsey, who started guiding under Waugh—and who would die in 1983 while guiding still for bear, a vessel bursting in his brain one spring day on Kodiak—and Bill Ambrosia, who learned his craft from his uncle Emil Ambrosia, who worked for both Charley and later his son Alf Madsen); but guides who made their names on the island are many—Talifson, Pinnell, Earl Stevens, and others—and only seem to call up a past that might almost have never been. A few years before his death in 1973, for example, Hal Waugh wrote in a letter that on one twelve-day hunt off Charley Madsen's 92-foot boat, sometime in the late forties, he counted 188 brown bear. Since 1960, however, he continued, he had never counted more than 110 in any three-hunt season. Which is probably very true, but still makes me believe, as I have for a long time, that there was always more game when we were younger, rain fell more lightly then, and the sun burned much brighter too.

If after all this that Cat operator or herring fisherman or airman, or whatever he may be, still insists upon his own private version of the Kodiak bear, then the only thing remaining to do is tell him to go to hell and get yourself off bear-hunting again at the first opportunity. That's what I would do, at any rate.

So in the first spring of the new decade I come back to Kodiak Island, as I knew I would. To a new bay—Spiridon—but again with

Bill Ambrosia. When I land on the gravel beach at the camp, Bill, his hair still black as a crow's wing, comes out of the hunting shack to greet me. My luck has not been good for a while, and I hope he can change that. I carry my gear across the grassy meadow above the beach and, as I am about to shake his hand, sink to my knees in an unseen boggy spot. Bill, having a smoke, looks down at me and shrugs. "Whenever they come back a second time," he announces in his low, husky voice, "I'm the one gets stuck with them."

He takes my gear and helps me up, then brings the spotting scope out of the shack and sets it up in a sunny spot so I may dry while looking through it. Adjusting the focus ring, Bill motions me over to see my first bears of this hunt. Their rumps dusted white, a sow and her three-year-old wrestle in powdery snow on the ridge far above us, their distant exertions silent in the scope lens. Mama bear grabs baby by the ear with her teeth and topples him over, mauling him affectionately for perhaps the last time in his life. In a matter of days she will drive him off so she can mate again. In spring, the bears come out of hibernation and, after dawdling sleepily around their dens for a few days, get real itchy, ready to rub off their winter coats and run down the mountain for salmon and sex. Ready, in short, to holler hi-de-ho.

I have yet to remember exactly how much the rock-hard beauty of Kodiak Island affected me the first time I was here, but in the next few days of hunting it all comes back. When I am not glassing for bear, I look first at the bald eagles. I try in vain to decide what their *screeing* most reminds me of: laughing oscilloscopes; the rusty top strand of a Waukegan-wire fence being pushed down; Martian fiddle music. I am fascinated by them until the day Bill and I come wide-open in the Whaler around a stony point and find fifteen or twenty fighting over the scraps of something dead on the dark beach. As we pass, the sky is filled suddenly with flapping raptors, a nation's symbols, so many behaving so ignobly at one time that I am far on the way to losing interest in them forever. Give me honest vultures any day.

The red foxes, though, with their orange miniature-wolf faces, black ears, and gold rings of eyes, are more to my, and Bill's, liking. One morning we land the skiff on a small island accessible by foot at low tide, and surprise a fox on its beach, come over earlier to dine on mussels. Seeing us, he bounds up the cliff and hides above. Bill, looking natty in a blue and white billed cap with a streamer fly hooked through the crown, says that foxes hate to swim. When low tide comes, I find Bill staring out at the exposed shoals and saying urgently to himself, "Go across now, fox. Go across."

Another time we see a female, I assume, apparently in some heat, strolling along the shore and making little steam-whistle toots as she squats frequently to mark her trail with urine. Rising daintily, she screams out just like someone being murdered and strolls on: the story, and the glory, of love.

Besides foxes, lines of the introduced Sitka blacktail patrol the shore; harbor seals pop their heads out of the bay with snorts, then dive with loud splashes; beaver and otter glide sleekly in the Spiridon River's estuary where every manner of waterfowl paddles; gulls circle, white and crying, in the air; but our attention is always drawn back to bear.

One afternoon on the little island we glass the bay's mountains from, we climb under a sea cliff to eat our lunches out of the rain. Somehow the uncommon occurrence of a boar eating a sow's cubs comes up in our mealtime conversation, and I suggest, trying to sound scientific without the least qualification for doing so, that perhaps by killing the sow's young the boar hopes to get her back into estrus *right now*. Bill Ambrosia thinks it over carefully before saying, "Maybe cubs are just good eating." We chew our Spam sandwiches meditatively, watching the Whaler bob below us on the end of its line, our rifles wrapped in a tarp in the bow as the rain pocks the bay.

We have seen hardly any tracks in the high snow yet, and those few we have seen all belonged to sows with cubs, leaving and entering dens near the mountain crests. Every day Bill awakes certain that we will have a boar by nightfall, but he also fears the bear are tardy this spring—perhaps because fall came later than usual and kept them out longer. He expects, he sighs, that any bear we see will be way up there in the snow, in the worst places to have to climb to. This is not malingering, just Bill getting older and the climbs not getting any easier. He will go as high as he has to for a bear and only makes the ascents more arduous in his head so when it comes time really to make them they will not seem so hard on his legs.

One morning we run out toward the mouth of the bay, looking with our binoculars for any tracks in the fresh snow at one of the bears' favored ridge crossings. Seeing none, and because the tides and wind are right for it, Bill plays a hunch and runs the Whaler full-throttle up the Spiridon River, skimming it around sandbars and boulders and submerged drift timber until we reach a set of rapids in a narrow canyon. Tying up the boat, we get our rifles and backpacks and head upriver for a mile or two along the high bank and over palisades above the water, moving through the dead grass and among alders, cottonwoods, and rose bushes. We can hear the rush of the river below us, and a great ball of sun burns through the mist above, clearing the sky for the first time in the hunt. The trail we follow has been cut twelve inches deep in places by the passage of Kodiak bear.

Soon we come to the foot of a good hill from which to glass the two mountain ranges running back out along either side of the bay, and we head for this hill's top. The river below us bends around sheer rock bluffs on one side of it—and on the other a large meadow of dead grass spreads to the foot of the rolling shoulders of hills mounting to the distant snow line and wind-carved crests—before winding out into a wide, flat valley running to the southeast. On the climb up the hill we find a bear track in the wet trail, too old to follow yet perfect in its way as a flower.

In the alders on top we sit all day, glassing the mountains. When I can stare at blank snow no longer, I watch a raven ride a thermal, tucking in his wings every so often and rolling over in the air, producing a soft, contented clucking. In cold wind under blue sky, I wonder how this obscure passion for Kodiak Island and its bear—a passion that has already taken up thousands of dollars and weeks of hunting—could possibly ever have gotten ahold of me. Yet I have only to recall that I have come here for nothing less than the largest and wildest trophy to be hunted in the wildest, largest land to hunt, and my passion seems not quite so obscure. My only wonder then is if my luck is about to change at last; but with the sun hot on my cap I sweated through on the climb, I realize that simply being here on a day like today is more than enough success for one lifetime—Kodiak bear or no Kodiak bear.

Then late in the afternoon of the 494th day since I last fired a shot at a big-game animal, I hear Bill Ambrosia whistle. I stand and hurry over to where he sits pointing to the rocky bluffs across from us, a Kodiak bear boar—something I did not expect to see today, or maybe ever—having just crossed over into view and working his way down through the bare cottonwoods to the riverbank, not a thousand yards distant. Bill watches him for a few minutes through his binoculars, then nods. As I am hurriedly stripping off gloves and raincoat, pulling the lens covers off my .300's scope, checking my belt loops for my extra shells, Bill, in no hurry at all, goes on watching the bear cross the river and begin working our way on top of the high bank on our side.

"Doesn't do any good to chase a bear," Bill says mildly from behind his binoculars. "He either has to lie down and you go up to him, or he comes right to you." The Kodiak bear moves on toward us, his big head rocking easily from side to side as he sways forward. "And since he's coming our way," Bill concludes, slipping his binoculars inside his patched parka and reaching for his .308, "we better go meet him."

We both stand and head down the hill. As we move through the long bent grass along the bank, I slip a round into the chamber and set the safety. Making it to a fallen cottonwood limb, I kneel behind it with Bill at my back and watch the bear come on. I am able to notice how cool and dry it has turned this afternoon, how pleasant the wind feels and the river sounds. In a moment or two I am going to kill a Kodiak bear, and an unbidden arrogant readiness fills me. I slip the safety off.

At thirty yards the bear climbs down into a tiny creek bed cutting into the bank and disappears. I start a count of the seconds, and at "four" he comes into sight again, having crossed over, and pauses above the creek to look off at the mountains.

"Behind the hump," Bill leans in to whisper to me. "Now."

The bear roars as my first shot breaks his shoulder and knocks him down into the creek bed. I work the bolt, and when he stands, as I was sure he would, and starts running toward the open yellow meadow, I take him in the same spot. He staggers, keeps moving, and my third shot enters his heart. He rolls over but rises one final time, and my last bullet into his chest pitches him forward where he lies still in the grass. It all takes much less than ten seconds, and he travels no more than twenty feet.

I reload fully before approaching him. Crossing the creek, I circle around behind him. I find his eyes open and already begin ning to cloud iridescent green. For an instant I feel what someone once called the "desolation of success": here before me, after so very long, is what I have come for. I unload my rifle and lean it against a cottonwood, then kneel beside the bear. I take in his full length, the massiveness of his hump and head, the long curve of his claws. He is an animal to humble the most wildly arrogant. I press my face into the warm fur along his great neck and for the first time smell the clean, sweet spring smell of Kodiak bear. Looking up, I see Bill's gapped yellow smile bright as sunlight, and my apprehension is dispelled like the mist.

This afternoon, only a few yards from where I now write, pale spring light falls through the doorway of the salting shed on Bill Ambrosia pouring a fifty-pound bag of salt over a big brown-bear hide and skull. Kneeling, Bill spreads the white salt over the white skin with his twisted and broken hands—hands that are the sum total of a lifetime of fishing, hunting, and guiding on Kodiak. He stands, hissing at the pain in his back from packing out the hide the day before. Brushing the salt from those hands, he looks at the hide. He takes a smoke from the pack and says to himself in his battered North Wind of a voice, "Now that should do it."

In the Territories

The Northwest Territories is an aqueous solution 1.3 million miles square, occupying the upper third of Canada. From the air, its sparsely treed terrain is so honeycombed with lakes, an overland route that would leave one dryshod looks impossible to pick. On maps of great detail, this extreme saturation makes the country resemble a cross section of gray porous tissue mounted on the blue-green glass of a microscope slide. On those same maps, the top of the Territories appears to be coming apart in the solution, sending hundreds and hundreds of islands—some vast, some small—floating upward into the polar ice.

The forceful pull of this wet northland is exerted on rivers far to the south of it, compelling them to turn away from the continent's more usual incline and flow on through Great Slave Lake to become one of the hemisphere's great rivers, the Mackenzie, before emptying into the arctic Beaufort Sea. Great Slave Lake itself is a vast body of fresh water, about 11,000 miles square and in places more than 2,000 feet deep. Although it is subarctic, in late June the sun will still only leave the territorial sky above it for a reluctant hour or so each night.

A fishing lodge sits here, where it has sat for the last seventeen years, on the lake's eastern arm near the village of Snowdrift, 115 air miles from Yellowknife. Here, besides the open waters of the lake, are also to be found islands and reefs and coves; Christie Bay, long and deep; Stark River—no more than a mile long, yet just possibly the finest stretch of American grayling water in the world; and Stark Lake, joined to Great Slave by the umbilical cord of Stark River but existing as a unique entity. All this takes place on the western edge of the Canadian Shield, and the surrounding Precambrian rock (some of the planet's oldest, an ancient ripple in the earth's mantle) bears the scars of glacial scouring—water as ice, having its way. You can see these scars as you pass close by the shore in your boat with your Chipewyan Indian guide, casting or trolling in some of the richest and most fragile of game fish waters, where lake trout, northern pike, and grayling fin beneath the icy surfaces.

My Indian guide was Fred Cassoway. His village of Snowdrift is an old Chipewyan settlement with a population of some two hundred. Its name frequently shows up without warning on world globes, holding down a single point of habitation in the Territories' wide emptiness. *Chipewyan* is a Cree term meaning "Pointed Skins" and refers either to the shape in which Fred's ancestors dried their beaver pelts or to the style in which they cut the tails of their caribou-hide shirts.

The life of those hide-wearing ancestors of Fred Cassoway's was a fierce one in a fierce land. For survival, they were dependent on spears, bone hooks, nets woven out of a rawhide thong known as *babiche,* and the timely migration of the caribou. They were edge-of-the-forest people who were repelled by the sight of barren tundra spreading north to the ice cap. They severely oppressed the neighboring Yellowknife and Dogrib Indians and were not always kind to their own women and aged. In one elegantly simple vision was contained their view of the afterlife and all they knew of religion: the dead would travel in a stone boat down a river to an island abounding in game; the good would land on that island; the evil would never reach it, sinking instead into the river to flounder in its dark waters forever. That the good had the added option of reincarnating again in the real world after reaching the island does not seem to have held much interest for the harsh Chipewyans.

Today, however, Fred Cassoway—forty years old and looking fit—is an amiable fellow who plays cautious blackjack on payday, traps a little in the winter, and guides sport fishermen after game species in the summer. One day I heard him singing some kind of lilting Chipewyan chant to himself as he piloted the boat, only to have the chant turn out to be, on closer hearing, a medley of country-and-western favorites, Hank Williams to Tompall Glaser. Another time I saw him sitting motionless in the stern, watching a tall billow of storm clouds, waiting for the thunder.

Just a few hundred yards east of the lodge, the mouth of Stark River is crossed by a rocky bar. The Chipewyan guides pick their route around this hazard in their twenty-horse outboards with all the restraint of Indy competitors picking their line down from the grandstand wall and into the first turn. Sometimes, perhaps *more* than sometimes, a prop becomes disengaged or the bottom of a motor is sheared away; but mostly the transit upriver is made without incident, though not without a qualm or two for the sport fisherman gripping the top of the gunwale with white-knuckled fists. In the first stretch of fast water above the bar, the schools of grayling can be seen leaping and rolling after insects. Here the anchor is dropped and the boat is tethered against the strong current. Besides props and motor bottoms, lying among the riverbed's stones is a wealth of lost anchors.

Once it had not been necessary to come this far north to find good grayling fishing. Once a place like the central Michigan town of Crawford could change its name to Grayling in celebration of the beauty and abundance of its local fish. But the grayling were too much a table delicacy for their own good and were fished back by nineteenth-century commercial interests until now the best American grayling fishing is to be found in far northern waters like this Canadian Stark River. Grayling in the five-pound class have come out of here, and two-pounders are not a rare sight. Charles, the current Prince of Wales, once journeyed to this river in search of grayling, and those who saw him angling in it accounted him a crackerjack fly fisherman. While not trying to take anything away from the bonny prince, I feel certain that had I grown up on the River Test or one of the other legendary chalk streams of England, I, too, would be something to see when I raised my split-bamboo rod.

As it was, I picked up my eight-foot graphite rod and used a technique that can most charitably be described as "unconventional." Having spent almost all my trip searching for a truly giant lake trout, I had neglected the grayling till my final day at the lodge, when I went out and, obeying some as yet unfathomable logic, rigged up my sinking line, tied a white-feathered jig to the end of it—which made the line cast like a logging chain—slapped it enervatedly into the river, watched the swift flow carry it straight back behind me, waited a moment, and set the hook on a grayling. Lord knows why such a procedure would work, but it did. And don't ask me what I thought I was doing, because I still don't know. The only thing I can say is that this odd behavior on my part was probably the result of the river's looking much too big and treacherous to wade, and my being pitiably clumsy when it comes to casting from a small boat: by the method I employed, all I had to do was dunk my line in the river, let it out, and catch a grayling.

Not that this method worked every time, of course, but often enough that I ended the day with a nice mess of fish, Fred Cassoway netting them as I brought them alongside, and I then just *having* to pick them up and lift their red-spotted dorsal fins—opened out like spinnakers—and see how the purple shaded across their large-scaled silvery bodies like the colors in a fog bow I had seen one cold morning on Christie Bay when we were lost in a mist. I also missed some fish, pulling the hook away from their small, though not soft, mouths before they could get around it; but I captured one sixteen-incher that went on the wall and enough of his tasty little brothers to make a fine meal.

My strange, dispirited angling of the last day might also have been brought on by my being somewhat fished out by then. I love fishing, I do not love it much more than eight and nine and ten full hours a day, seven days in a row, however. (If I wanted to work, I'd get a job—a *real* one.) I think the thrill peaked for me sometime during my sixth day on the water when we were in a grassy little pond near a place in Great Slave Lake called Murky Lake. We had come over an hour from the lodge to the end of a small cove where we then had to portage the heavy aluminum boat across a tiny isthmus, rolling it along a conveyor of smooth logs laid across the ground, and into a large bay, where we powered up a shallow inlet filled with ducks and into the one-acre pond. I fished with my spinning outfit in that opaque brown water for most of the morning. The sun was warm and the air was thick with neon-blue damselflies and enormous pestering horseflies. And every cast—quite literally—of my spoon brought either a hookup or a strike until it became completely embarrassing.

I certainly did love those pike, though, those jacks, those water wolves, those "nasty snake fish," as Fred Cassoway happily dubbed them. How could anyone not love so vengeful, wicked, and saurian-looking a creature, with its white belly and green-whorled back, its ugly jumble of raking teeth, its low-slung bill like the hood of a Corvette, its dorsal fin set impossibly far back on its fuselage, and the diligent manner in which it lurks among the swaying pipes of water grass, waiting to kill something? That great surge of energy when they strike, and then when they see the boat, is a marvelous thing. I must have caught and released scores of pike that sixth day, until it was just too much. Therefore, it is an earlier day I remember more fondly.

It was at the falls on Snowdrift River, which comes all the way from the "bare land in the north," as Fred Cassoway told me, to flow into Stark Lake. We went up the river, past the wooden crosses in the old graveyard high on the bank, then skimmed over the low water below the falls. There was a big shoulder of dry black rock beside the falls, and I scrambled out onto it and started to cast. The first time I threw out a lure, the pike followed it in groups of two or three right back to the rocks and stared up balefully out of the water at me and the lure as it dangled dripping in the air above them. Then I cast again, trying to pitch the spoon into the edge of the foam the green spill of water beside me was making in the river, and I was into a pike. While I fought it, a friend fishing with me landed a very fine one, its body deeply gashed from its struggle to climb the falls in defiance of gravity. I landed mine, then went after more. At last, after I'd thrown all the lures I had at those pike, they came to recognize them for what they were and refused to take any more, leaving me no choice but to climb into the boat and float back down the Snowdrift and into Stark Lake.

During the seven days of fishing, I trolled for lake trout all over Stark Lake, eastern Great Slave Lake, Murky Lake, Christie Bay, around Fortress Island, and through the Gap—where one of the Chipewyan guides whipped out his .30-30 and dropped a cow moose on the shore, creating a brief hiatus in the angling while the other guides sped over and assisted him in butchering her out. Beyond the Gap we trolled even as far as Wildbread Bay, one of Great Slave Lake's farthest perimeters. At its best, most trolling amounts to what the Italian language knows as *dolce far niente,* a delicious inactivity: the Slow Boat to China Syndrome. At its worst, a sport fisherman in a small open boat begins to see his shadow no longer merely gliding over the water, but descending and diffusing into it, seeming to trail away and dissipate until he begins to feel there may soon be not only nothing left of his shadow, but nothing left of himself.

On the other hand, there are rare times and places when trolling can be highly rewarding, as when you can catch fourteen lake trout (actually a char) in a single day, amounting to at least a hundred pounds of *Salvelinus namaycush,* and then go out and catch thirteen more the day after. In all those places I named above, I boated lake trout, even catching a couple just by casting out and reeling in while the boat was dead in the water and Fred Cassoway was wiping it up after netting and releasing one of my fish. Even in Stark River, I threw out a little French Mepps on my spinning outfit to see what kind of grayling might go for it, and wound up with an eight-pound trout—something of a disappointment, since I believed I was in the process of wrestling the new all-tackle without-a-doubt world-record grayling to the boat.

All the trout were netted and released except for the two I took home to eat and the trout I'd have for shore lunch. At noon, Fred Cassoway would carry the food box up from the bow of the boat, make a stone fire ring on the gravel beach, build a squaw-wood fire in it, set the blackened skillet and white shortening on the wire grill, fillet the just-caught trout on an oar blade, flour and fry up the fillets while the beans and potatoes cooked and the billy of strong tea boiled above the pale yellow flames and the sport fisherman sipped a can of cold Canadian lager.

When I bought my spoons at the lodge's tackle shop— purchasing every manner of five-o'-diamonds and seven-spot and red-and-white and fire-orange Troll Devle and Rok't-Devlet and No. 5 Canadian Charger—I took them down first thing to the repair shed on the boat dock and borrowed the mechanic's pliers to press down all the barbs on the hooks.

"Thank you," I said, handing him back his pliers.

"No, sir," he said, taking them from me. "It is always my pleasure to see a sportsman doing that."

After a short time of fishing in these waters you could begin to tell the size of the trout at the end of your wire leader by the way it fought, the smaller ones thrashing and flailing, the bigger ones— the old, sometimes forty-year-old, slow-growing ones of this frigid lake—taking out line in a straight pull and holding it firm down deep. You could imagine their large heads, wide as shovel blades, the sharp hooked teeth in their jaws, their forked coppery tails swinging gently but powerfully.

The one I remember best, of course—don't we always?—is the big one that got away. It was my very first afternoon on Stark Lake, right after a lake-trout-chowder lunch eaten in the lodge under illustrations of red-coated Mounties hanging on the walls, and we were trolling around a little island with a gimpy stand of spruces on it.

"No fish," Fred Cassoway announced after a quarter-hour of circling the island. He pointed off across the blue water toward another island he wanted to try; and as he started for it, the Len Thompson No. 4 I was reeling in snagged the bottom of the lake.

"Snagged," I called to Fred Cassoway above the noise of the outboard. He nodded and reversed the motor, and when I got over the snag, the bottom of the lake began to move, swimming slowly and unmistakably away. I fought that bottom of the lake on my too-light eight-pound monofilament for the next fifty minutes. Sometimes I would pump it up almost to the surface. Fred Cassoway, leaning far over the gunwale and peering into the water, would catch sight of it and pronounce with deep solemnity the words "Oh shit." I was too busy at such times, trying to hang on to the bottom of the lake as it labored to pull me overboard, to see much more than the flash of a very bright wide tail as it drove something huge back down into the water.

After almost an hour, the bottom of the lake still hung immobile ten feet under the boat as I strained to budge it one inch. Then I saw that I had been cranking away so furiously and futilely against my reel's drag that the line had begun to twist and kink. And finally it parted and the trout was gone, and I was just sitting there, drifting on Stark Lake, drifting above ancient, and not quickly replaceable, fish, drifting silently in the Territories.

I was a man waiting for a flood. Or was I hoping for one? On the rusty hills across from me I could see the runnels the floods of past seasons had cut through the tundra, as if that tundra had been raked by the claws of something impossibly large. If that flood came again, it would first swell beyond the land's capacity to contain it here, on this plateau north of the 57th parallel, then flow over the crests of those hills and down the rocks and through the sedge and berries, through the stands of spruce, and into the George River. That flood, in its winter's pelage of hollow guard hairs, would then breast the swift current and climb out onto this side, to flow out into country of large lakes and wide valleys beyond, before pooling around the southern rim of Baie d'Ungava. This was a flood which, if it came, would proceed in a click-footed progression.

In its fall migration, that is what the George River caribou herd most assuredly is: a flood, a flood of seasonable yet unpredictable course. Once, though, not so many years ago, it was far more trickle than deluge. Here in the Ungava (Northern Québec)–Labrador region of Canada, there were few caribou to be found during all the first half of this century. The herd seems to have crashed sometime toward the end of the 1800s, for a variety of speculative reasons, and on its own took five decades and better to rebuild. By the late 1950s a herd of 15,000 animals or so could, with luck, be seen; by the early sixties 40,000 to 60,000 would be found. In the autumn of 1975 (as reported in a paper on the caribou written by one Ian Juniper and published by Québec's Ministère du Loisir, de la Chasse et de la Pêche) the George River herd numbered over 176,000 animals and was growing, and today it is probably the largest caribou herd roaming North America. What I wanted to see this autumn, then, was that herd in its full, jittery migration. I had come to Ungava to see it flowing over the hills in such volume that it would no longer seem that it was the caribou who were in transit over the rolling tundra, but that the tundra itself was running under the caribou, like a leg sliding beneath a wide warm blanket of gray.

I went to Ungava in mid-September of 1982, to the town of Schefferville. Schefferville sits at the end of the line, railroad and otherwise. Industry has forsaken it, but it still serves as the staging ground for the many caribou camps dotting the banks of the Fleuve George, many miles to the northeast. For the Scheffervillians, September would seem to be the one month they have for making the entire year's nut. That is the month when large numbers of the most well known and well heeled of the international hunting community make *their* annual fall migration through the country, searching—and not always by the strictest of fair chase means—for that grail of the world's record Québec–Labrador (as Boone & Crockett calls the animal) caribou bull, sowing money as they pass. Stand in the tiny drab glass-walled terminal of the Schefferville airport for the briefest of times in September, and you are likely to be able to put more faces to famous names than you could, or would absolutely care to, shake a stick at.

This mid-September, when I had passed through Schefferville

and come at last, by light aircraft, then small rubber boat, to stand by this river, was not the first time I had gone to find caribou. That had been fourteen years before, and I had not hunted them since, though I am hard pressed to say why not. Certainly the caribou has always fascinated me in the extreme.

Many people do not consider the caribou very handsome, or very smart ("Plankton eaters!" I once heard somebody sum them up). Well, at least I, for one, believe them to be quite *handsome*. But maybe the caribou's primary fascination for me comes from its living so far north in that, to me, most charming of country—"charming" as in a shaman's spell, or curse—the country of the Subarctic and Arctic and even *beyond*. Robert E. Peary, as he quested for the pole, noted that the nearly snow-white caribou, the smallest of all, to which he gave his name, was to be found as high up as the 83rd degree of latitude! Or maybe it's just that the caribou are the final great *herds* of anything at large in North America. Maybe it's because that as a circumpolar people—we who are mostly northern European, or those of us who are northern Asian, or northern North American Indian—we have hunted and lived off the caribou for some forty thousand years, eating his meat, wearing his hides, fashioning our tools from the candelabra of his antlers, transferring his image from our yeasty bicameral brains to the cool rock of our cave walls. And maybe why I had not gone back to hunt another sooner was because I still remembered that first one so well, and feared to tamper with the pleasure of that memory.

I had been sixteen, and before leaving for the Talkeetna Mountains of Alaska I had walked into the barber's and told him to shear my hair away to a fine burr. This was, to be sure, an odd request for a callow Southern Californian youth to be making in the troubled Year of Our Lord 1968, but I now believe it was one that secretly did the barber's heart a world of good. I think I wanted at the time to be free of anything superfluous that I felt might get in the way of my purpose of becoming a *hunter*. (I could have even thought, way back somewhere, I was receiving a kind of tonsure.) All I *know* today, when I confront photos of myself from that period, is that I have no actual idea what the hell it was I thought I was up to, aside from having all my hair hacked off, of course.

So some days later, with a cold wind passing over my scalp and a tremble from something more than just the chill passing through my muscles, I bellied over the heathered rim of a small basin, at whose bottom there lay bedded a barren-ground caribou bull, and put a .30-caliber bullet through his heart. I got the antlers and cape and some of the meat out that day; but when I returned for the rest it was gone, gotten by grizzlies.

That was my only caribou, as well as my first big-game animal ever, and to this day I could not tell you which of Alaska's many barren-ground herds he was a member of. The Delta? The Mentasta? The Nelchina? Across Canada there spread more great herds of barren-ground caribou: the Porcupine and Kaminuriak; Wager Bay; Baffin; the Beverly, the Bathurst, and the Bluenose. Does that make the George River caribou herd, then, the greatest of the barren-ground? The various schools of thought on this are not without interest.

North America is considered to be home for basically two types of caribou, the barren-ground and the woodland. Their names alone should explain that the essential difference between the two is one of the relative habitat of each, with the woodland forming smaller and less migratory herds. All caribou, and the Old World reindeer as well, are part of the *Rangifer tarandus* species. Some experts choose to place the George River herd in the woodland caribou's subspecies of *Rangifer tarandus caribou.* A pretty much archaic classification, from a time when there were not only recognized to be barren-ground, mountain, woodland, and Newfoundland caribou, but Osborn's, Grant's, Greenland, and Stone's in the bargain, has the herd's members being called the Labrador barren-ground caribou, *Rangifer arcticus caboti.* John P. Kelsall, author of the first-rate *The Migratory Barren-Ground Caribou of Canada,* puts all this business of labels into apt perspective by justly pointing out that thus far attempts at simplifying the specifications for caribou—as with the numerous attempts at explaining the reasons for the clicking sound their walk produces—"have left much to be desired," and later goes on to encourage us "interested readers" to take a good look at the available literature and "draw personal conclusions."

Accepting Kelsall's most generous offer, I would say that in my opinion the caribou of Ungava-Labrador, while being apparently as large as woodland caribou, and possessing a similar color, at the same time *do* live above timberline where they are active migrants over the tundra. Which, of course, settles nothing. So I will be content to turn to the early Algonquins, who called the animal graphically *mekālixpowa,* the "snow shoveler," or to the Micmacs, who knew him to be *xalibu,* "the pawer," for his penchant for scraping through the snow with his hooves to feed. It will be my personal conclusion to call him—caribou.

Now I watched caribou's cows and calves lift those wide hooves—wider than they are long—and trot slack-jawed across the tundra around me. There was a warm south wind back here above the George; too warm. The bare rolling tundra shimmered with heat. The caribou were not coming to the river in any numbers in this weather, and my bearded Québecois guide François and my Mississippian hunting friend Fred Fortier and I had left the river to climb up the talus of treacherously loose rock along its bank, then over more glacier-scoured rock farther up—where white-turning ptarmigan clattered away from us—and at last onto a slope above a valley with a lake of cold sweet water—where geese swam—on its floor. This is where we sat my first full day of caribou-hunting in the Ungava, glassing, swatting at blackflies, and watching the cows and calves run in their erratic, nearly exhausted trajectories, trying to elude the insects.

The weather was the kind you'd expect to find in June in some place very much farther south. The Subarctic can, in fact, often experience summer temperatures into the eighties, then down again into the minus-sixties come winter—subjecting the caribou to a temperature range of over 150 degrees between highs and lows. In this warm weather now the blackflies came out in full force. Few sights are more disheartening in this life than that of blackflies bathing in the meniscus of nearly pure N, N-diethyl-meta-toluamide at the top of your opened bottle of insect repellant. Especially when they actually seem to be *frolicking* in the stuff.

Unlike the warble fly—who lays her eggs in the caribou's underhair, and whose larvae when they hatch bore through the caribou's skin and migrate beneath it to the back area where they cut breathing holes and remain developing for ten months or so, reaching the size of the ball of your thumb before falling to the ground to pupate—the blackfly lays her eggs in swift, clean, well-oxygenated turbulent water such as that carried by the George. She lives *off* the caribou—and anything else warm-blooded, including me and you—not *on* him. She (since only the females bite) is known in entomological circles as a "pool feeder" who inflicts her bites with a scissorlike movement of her mandibles, then enlarges the wounds by forcing her maxillae into them so she can *then* insert her labrum-epipharynx and, one must suppose, *lap* the blood that wells forth. The bite itself seems quite painless when she delivers it: at least in my case. Before I heeded François's advice and began lashing my pants cuffs closed with my bootlaces, the blackflies, without my being aware of it, tattooed a bright garland of tiny red rose buds around each of my ankles above my boot tops. Even now, months later, the ring of scars persists.

Far from being a mere annoyance, blackflies can kill. In 1923 they were implicated in the deaths of 20,000 head of domestic animals in southeastern Europe. On the tundra, four-hundred-pound caribou, to escape the torment of these tiny insects, will "gad" about berserkly, sometimes fracturing limbs in the process. The flies can distract the caribou from the task of feeding to the point that they die of starvation. Blackflies can, as can other factors, alter the migration route of whole herds of caribou. Finally, blackflies can simply drain enough blood from a caribou that he lies down and dies of anemia. Little wonder then, that, as one of the Québecois guides—speaking like Tonto on the Champs-Élysées—explained to one of the other hunters, "Many flies, no caribou; *no* flies, *many* caribou." Now, in this mid-September time of unseasonable warmth, I would have to keep my face to the wind to prevent my inhaling blackflies. We saw no bull caribou in the valley with the lake that day.

The next day we waited again for the caribou by the river. For the Eskimo—known by that name to the Cree as "he who eats meat raw," but to themselves quite rightly as Inuit, "the people"—and other northern tribes, waiting by the river, whatever its name, for the caribou to cross is a time-honored ritual. Along the approaches over the tundra to the traditional crossings the Eskimos would build lines of stone cairns, called *inuksuit* (meaning "resembling a person"), the piles of rock made to look like hunters. The Eskimos would place moss on the tops of the cairns to create the illusion of hair, or attach sticks to them to look like weapons. Sometimes live hunters would station themselves between the cairns to heighten the effect. The caribou, seeing this phalanx of armed men, would be channeled down to where the rest of the hunters waited by the river to ambush the herd at the spearing point. As for Fred and me, we could take it for just that one day, sitting by the river in the warm sun, watching the blackflies mantle us in a motile garment of insect, while only caribou calves and cows in dribs and drabs came over the treeless ridge across from us and in that ground-eating trot of theirs made their way to the water and swam across. Then we had to go up onto the crest of something the next day.

In the morning, as François, Fred, and I made our way up from the river, the wind had switched around to the northwest and was lacing us with wet snow. We made our way up over the stones to a long ridge and followed it out some miles to where we could look down on the wide stark valley of a stream running into the George. The stream looked as though it were flowing on the moon back here, this far north of the tree line. François found a sheltered spot beside some stunted fir trees and made a fire to boil tea and toast sandwiches on. Fred and I sat and glassed. The stream valley ran a very long ways, a silver thread laid across brown tundra. This was caribou weather, flyless and wet, yet still that flood was not coming. Fred got to his feet after a while and slung his cut-down .375, his old bear gun and a far cry from my .270, over his shoulder and marched away to find whatever was to be found. An hour and a half later he was back, flopping down onto the heather and announcing to the world that there were no caribou of any description to be found *anywhere* around here. Which was the precise moment two caribou cows chose to top a small ridge a few yards from us and just stand there, staring at us with the same sort of keen "with it" expression I had come to associate with the African hartebeest, that simplest of all the earth's antelope—at least the simplest-*looking*. They went on staring for a spell, then clopped past us and went up the valley along the ridgeline, their abbreviated antlers silhouetted against the gray sky.

Nature, or *whatever,* has been so profligate in bestowing antlers upon the caribou species, even the cows come equipped with them—the only members of the deer family whose females are so endowed. Like snowflakes, no two sets of caribou antlers are ever exactly alike, and almost never will one of a caribou's antlers be the mirror image of his other. With their "anteriorly extended brow and bez tines . . . [and] posteriorly ascending main beam which is distally semi palmate and which may have subsidiary posterior tines" (according to Kelsall), the shoveled antlers of a caribou are an elaboration of almost ludicrous proportions. One wonders what such International Stylists as Walter Gropius, Mies van der Rohe, or the inimitable (and constantly imitated) Le Corbusier, with their intense architectural love of cleanly wrought parallelepipeds and uninterrupted horizontal planes, would have made of the extravagant Art Nouveau, the *stile floreale,* design of caribou antlers. I imagine them all clustered out on the tundra, clenching the stems of their functionally formed pipes between their gritted teeth and shaking their heads in bitter incomprehension at the unrelenting forest of all that sweeping, multipointed bone matter before them. Those antlers are audacious monuments to the exorbitant. And they'll all be shed before summer, truly showing up the natural world—which could be improvident enough to make in such numbers an animal as improbable as the caribou to begin with—for the flagrant wastrel it is.

I would not be here until summer, though. I was scheduled to have only four full days of hunting, and now there was a plane coming for me. I would have only a few hours more in which to be in the right place when a trophy bull came. That last morning, after our day on the ridge, we jounced upriver over the white spraying rapids in our small rubber boat and found a crossing to wait at during the time we had left. Other boats came past and disappeared around a bend. The weather was all bad now, and I felt that that flood I had been hoping for could not be very far off. In a short time I heard shots echoing down the canyon of the George River, then all those little gray boats that had gone by before began coming back with their loads of great antlers. They had caught the beginnings of the surge upriver somewhere, but I was left just to sit along the bank and watch them go on by, making for the lodge.

A day or two, it seems, can make all the difference in the hunt for migratory caribou if the herd begins to mass and move, but this, I'm afraid, was not going to be the day for me. At the end of it, being in a slightly wrong place at a slightly wrong time, I would have to give up my wait by the river and make my way back down it, over the rapids pounding hard on the boat's bottom, through the chill rain flying at me.

No fall comes with a money-back guarantee on when or where, or even if, the George River caribou herd, or any caribou herd anywhere, will make its way across the river. Being a flood of animals, there is always a chance of its unaccountably choosing a new course to follow, a different time to run. But if the flood does come with, they say, as many as three hundred bulls a day fording the waters and the land behind them aswarm with thousands of cows and calves crowding down, to those lucky enough to see it, it must resemble a tsunami wave breaking on a shore, or the aurora borealis swirling around the polar cap. I think just being there to see that someday would be enough for me. Someday I would like to occupy the exact point in Ungava at which that flood crests and have it flow around me. Or even to let it pick me up and carry me off. Probably far worse things can occur to you than to be swept away in a tide of mammals—to go with it and discover where it will carry you, to remember with new pleasure a time above the 57th.

Grizzlyland

No man, the Pomo Indians of California believed, had earned the right to hunt the grizzly bear before he reached the age of thirty. So in the spring of my thirtieth year I resolved to go north to hunt *Ursus arctos horribilis* for the first time.

I went to hunt the grizzly in the spring because that is when the bear's hide, barring rubbed patches, will still be in the prime of deepest winter, thick and silver-tipped. The big boars emerge from the dens first in the spring, ahead of the sows and cubs, and commence their roaming search for feed to replace all the body fat they lost to hibernation. Theodore Roosevelt estimated that fully half of the numerous grizzlies he took during his long career as a huntsman in North America were simply *happened* onto while he was out after something else; and in the fall this is unquestionably how many grizzlies *are* taken, a bear tag becoming a sort of lottery ticket sheep and caribou hunters purchase on the chance that during their mixed-bag hunt they may top out over the rim of some open basin on a chill September afternoon and accidentally discover a bear ardently unearthing a chipmunk, turning over square yards of tundra with his long curved white claws in hopes of realizing one single ounce of meat. In the spring, though, there are only bears to hunt, and the only luck you will have will be the kind you make for yourself. Your sole reason for being here in the spring is grizzly.

The proper way to enter grizzly country is on the back of a horse, and my horse's name was Shorty. Imagine a beer-wagon Clydesdale somehow stunted out of his last six hands of rightful growth, and you will have a fair notion of Shorty. He was an employee of the young outfitter Cal Smith of Pink Mountain, 143 miles from Fort St. John up the dust-choked, windshield-busting Alaska Highway in northeastern British Columbia. Cal's hunting area spreads east to the Alberta border, and south across the drainage of the Beatton River, which flows grayly through densely timbered willow and poplar and jack pine country down to the Peace. This green country is colored as well by the rusting metal around gas-well sites and by the yellow of seismic lines—trails scalped dead true across the hills in winter by the wide blades of Caterpillar tractors, providing geologists with the access their mechanized testing equipment needs to come in and search for more natural gas. There are signs of men almost anywhere you care to look (though in over two weeks I saw not one stranger), so much so you would never think grizzlies would inhabit such a place; but they do.

When Shorty and I rode into this country it was the middle of May and the snow was falling in heavy wet flakes among the jack pines. Ahead of me, leading a young pack horse, rode Ray Watkins, Cal Smith's assistant guide and best friend since their days together as hot-rodding and hockey-playing teenagers on the wheat prairies of Saskatchewan. Riding silently in the dark timber, we came to a stringer with snow piled on its banks and jumped our horses across. When I cleared, I looked back and watched Mickey on the black gelding jump across with the other pack horse, an untried mare. The pack horse stumbled, her unshod rear hoof slipping into the icy water of the narrow feeder creek, and Mickey had to pull her out, the mare's eyes wide with momentary panic. Mickey was Ray's wife, a tall, slender Dutch girl whose love of the wild had led her first to the Camargue horse lands in France, then to live among Spanish Gypsies, then to the Colorado Rockies, and at last all the way to this wildest corner of the New World, where she met and fell in love with and wed a trapper and hunting guide.

We came out of the timber and rode onto a seismic line. The ground was wet and muddy, and the horses didn't much care for it. They tried to keep to the edges where the ground was less soft, and where you had to be forever reining them away from overhanging branches. (Give a horse a trail *two miles* wide and he'll *still* wind up trying to tightrope down the last twelve-inch ribbon of dry edge.)

Along with us trotted the Watkinses' black Lab pup Tammy, trotting right under the horses' hooves until one of them had quite enough and I watched Tammy cartwheel, yowling, through the air—only to get up, shake herself off, and trot happy-go-luckily right back up to the horses. The worth of dogs and horses in grizzly country, by the way, can be infinite. As you ride down a trail, there is always the possibility of a bear standing around the next bend, munching on some tasty dead thing he has just discovered. Usually if one *is* there, you won't know about it unless you find his tracks, because he will be more than pleased to clear out should he wind you or hear you coming. But if he fails to, then your dog, suddenly halting and stiffening, his ears pricking up, or your horse, pulling up short and snorting loudly, will tell you that while here there may not necessarily be dragons, it's a damned good bet there be bears!

A little before noon we all turned off the seismic line and rode out a trail cut through windfallen poplar trees. The campsite stood in a clearing on the brow of a hill at the top of a long ridge snaking down to a creek with no name. The creek fed into the Beatton, and where they joined there was a large open meadow covered in moose-cropped willow bushes. It looked like any sort of north country meadow—unless you knew the kind of place a bear would come to, then you recognized it at once for what it could only be: a *bear* meadow. Our camp was at a natural lookout above it, and here we were to stay for fourteen days.

We built a fire before anything else. Some logs were already lashed between two jack pines and made a frame where we set up the Baker tent I would be sleeping in. While snow hissed into the yellow flames, we raised that slanted-roof cook tent, with the asbestos-shielded hole in the wall where a stovepipe was supposed to go—only there was no stove and during our time in camp all our cooking would be done over the fire's coals. After my tent was up, and the dirt floor covered, first with trimmed spruce boughs, then two thick saddle blankets and a tarp, with my sleeping pad and down bag rolled out on top of this, I helped Ray and Mickey put up their white wall tent.

The snow lifted. By the time we had camp made, it was late afternoon. All day I'd been hearing a sound like a vague but insistent heartbeat everywhere around me in the country. As we sat on the wooden panniers, eating steaming bowls of moose stew Mickey had canned from the bull Ray killed the preceding fall, I heard the sound once more, very near. Now it sounded to me like a multicolored bowling ball being dribbled on a hardwood lane.

"Grouse," Mickey said, stirring the blackened skillet set on the blackened wire grill.

I stood and walked to the edge of the clearing, spoon and orange plastic bowl in hand, and looked down into the timber to see a ruffed grouse standing on a dead log. He was a dozen feet away, and as I watched him, eating my supper, he stood erect on the log, fanning his tail down and raising his ruff and topknot. He lifted his wings and, at first hesitantly, began to drum them against his chest. He picked up the tempo, the drumming becoming bolder, until his wings were a blur and the sound became a constant *thrum*. Then the cock bird slowed and stopped and slumped back down.

Before all the light was gone I went out ten yards from camp, to where the ridge ran up from the nameless creek, and glassed the meadow below for bear. This far north, this time of year, you could, with good binoculars, very nearly find enough illumination to stay out all "night" glassing. But by ten or ten-thirty it was just obscure enough that you could, with a relatively clear conscience, draw the line.

As I walked back into camp, a hen grouse flew up into a poplar and began to pluck off the new buds. The cock grouse appeared then, his ruff like the black mane of a lion and his raised tail spread open. He strutted right in front of me, not giving a damn, and posed under the tree while the hen, the slim branch bending precariously under her weight, went right on feeding, obviously not giving a damn either.

On my way to my tent I noticed that Ray had strategically picketed the horses around the camp, to prevent, as he put it, "surprises" during the night. I thought about this as I was climbing into my sleeping bag. I got my .375 H. & H. Magnum, and as Lewis and Clark's men had been ordered to do with their guns during their expedition's sojourn in bear country, lay down with it beside me and fell soundly asleep.

That was my first day in grizzlyland. Others followed.

Hunting grizzly is a game requiring far more mental stamina—in the form of a vast, almost transcendental patience—than physical. (Maybe that's why the Pomos wanted their hunters to wait till thirty, when the coltish restlessness of youth, which makes one crave only *action* and *more* action, had died out some, leaving them better prepared for the possible long haul of finding that one bear in all that big country.) The country bears live in can be rough, of course. But not that rough. Any reasonably fit individual, especially with horses, can get into the worst of it. What cannot be gotten into so easily, however, is the grizzly's nature.

A century's worth of confrontational politics between him and high-power repeating rifles has turned the bear from a reportedly daylight rambler into a midnight skulker. He has learned caution and circumspection, but most people who know him well agree that this in no way means he may have likewise learned cowardice. A boar on a kill or, most particularly, a sow with cubs will *not* at all costs flee from men. Any man foolhardy enough to approach too near to these kinds of grizzly—or *any* kind of grizzly, for that matter—should account himself lucky if he somehow manages to live to regret it.

The bear's adopted reserve can make hunting him a long process of waiting for him to show. In the province of British Columbia this wait is compounded by the fact that you may not set out bait to attract him in to you. In the spring, though, not even bait would be a sure thing. A problem with spring hunting is hitting a time neither too early nor too late, a time when the bears have begun to move away from their dens in the deep cover and started to feed on open hillsides and in the meadows, but not so late that they have also begun to rub off their fur. There are hunters who believe that early in the spring a bear will not show much interest in dead meat and will bypass winter-killed carcasses until he has got his stomach functioning again on a diet of fresh roots and berries. These hunters contend, though, that he will remember where the meat was and return for it later. (A grizzly ranks very far down on the scale of productive carnivores, by the way. His abilities as a food gatherer lend themselves to grazing and rooting, first; scavenging, second; and the rare and inefficient predation on big and small game, third. He is a splendid omnivore, though, and as John Muir noted, "to him almost everything is food, except granite.")

From our lookout less than ten yards out of camp, Ray and I would each take a shift in the morning, glassing the meadow and surrounding woodland country. There was a well-worn bear trail that ran up from the Beatton and across the meadow, then entered a stand of leafless poplars on the hillside just below our camp and crossed over the foot of the ridge and continued up the winding canyon of the nameless creek until canyon and trail and creek all played out in a willow marsh. Our firm belief was that if we could just make ourselves watch the trail long enough, morning and evening, a bear would appear on it. Almost as if, though not quite, by magic—the "magic" being no more than patience and single-minded determination. So at four-thirty each morning I would be lying out on the hill, watching the frost build up on the tarp I had wrapped around me, seeing feeding moose gliding glacially across the meadow, their long legs hidden in the willows, hearing honkers flying along the river in mated pairs, noticing a beaver slicing a wake across the meadow pond's glassy surface. It was of signal importance both to make the watching a meditative end in itself—to keep from going utterly dipsy—and yet be fully prepared for the instantaneous apparition of a bear below. That is how a bear comes: one second only a wall of trees is visible, the next there is a bear outside that wall, shambling your way.

One morning while I was glassing, an animal trotted into view from out of nowhere, crossing the meadow. My heart began to beat like that grouse's drumming as I fumbled to get the animal focused in my binoculars. It halted behind a willow bush with its head down, sniffing. Its fur was charcoal-colored and the wind made it bristle.

Small black bear, I thought, dismissing it. Then it lifted its head and tail and my heart took off again. Wolf.

No matter what some folks may think of wolves—a popular bumper sticker in that small corner of British Columbia ever so sardonically comments on the seemingly uncontrollable population boom in the predators by declaring, *"EAT MOOSE—5,000 Wolves Can't Be Wrong,"* which may even be an *under*statement—there is no animal more indicative of the wild. When you see wolves, you can be certain you've gotten about as far away from things as you're going to get.

I watched the wolf trot on and disappear into the poplars. For some reason, call it instinct if you like, I knew exactly where I could find him next. Without waking Ray, I slipped down the ridge toward the nameless creek. About a hundred yards from the bottom the slope of the ridge turned up and made a little knob before continuing down. Here the poplars ended on one side of the ridge, and on the other was open hillside. I slunk to this knob and on hands and knees crept over it. By the edge of the creek the wolf stood, pawing at the dirt and sniffing it. His weight looked all forward in his chest and shoulders, and behind them the ribs were beginning to show through his coat. I raised my binoculars to see him better—falling victim to one of the major fallacies of modern times, that being that we somehow see "better" through the precision-machined glass of binoculars and cameras and microscopes than we do through our unaided eyes: we *may* see more; we do *not* see better—and catching the glint of the lenses, the wolf looked up at me with his depthless lupine eyes and then stepped unhurriedly out of sight into the poplars. He had no idea what I might be, but he meant to find out. So I just stood there, waiting for a wolf, as if it were something I did every day. When I saw him again he was halfway up from the river to me, having stalked up through the trees. By now, though, he knew what I was; and when I saw him he was coming out of the trees like a streak of black, his tail shot straight out behind him, heading up the canyon for parts unknown. He'd been hungry enough to make sure I was more or less inedible before giving up on me. The sight of him, though, left behind food that filled my very soul.

After an hour or two of glassing in the morning, then, I would wake Ray, and while he glassed I would crawl back into my bed. Mickey would have breakfast ready around eight, then Ray and I, and sometimes Mickey and Tammy, too, would saddle up and ride off to hunt for sign of grizzly bear.

Our riding turned up precious little of it, though. For a while all we could find was some tracks of a moderate-sized bear around an old well site where he had been digging at the tuberous flowers.

"Coltsfoot," Mickey called them as she rode by, reminded of the flora of her native Holland (though they were pink flowered and something North American like spring beauty). Mickey caught up to Ray, and as I looked on in mute horror, that refined, polite, charming, *European* young woman, her hair neatly done up in a red bandanna, bummed a pinch of Beechnut chewing tobacco off her husband and packed it away.

On our rides we would find the shed antlers of moose, lying palmated and white, everywhere we went, though especially in boggy meadows, and we would put them up on bushes or in trees to act as signposts. Once we jumped a very much *live* moose out of a bog deep in some timber and heard him go striding away over the wet land with a sound like an extremely large stationary diesel engine, its great flywheel whirling, tearing loose from the steel deck of a tramp freighter and sliding off into a storm-tossed green ocean. One afternoon a pair of coyotes, their fur long and silvery, made a half-hearted jogging hunt after us down a seismic line, but soon abandoned the undertaking when we kept turning around in our saddles and catching them *in flagrante delicto,* as it were—causing them to halt and start staring off into space, the picture of innocence. Another day Ray glanced off the trail and saw a big lynx sitting tall on a downed log fifteen feet away, sunning himself where the light fell among the shadows of the trees. Ray pointed to him as we rode past; then we turned and rode back to look at him again and he remained where he was, staring at us blankly with his tabby's face, never having seen a man on horseback before. In all, I saw four lynx, four coyotes, three wolves, mountain caribou, mule deer, innumerable moose, and three black bears on the hunt. There were, in addition, reliable reports of mountain goats, wood bison, and wild horses also running in that country, and there were times when the sight of mastodon passing by would have come as no surprise.

It was fast becoming apparent, however, that this spring was going to be a late arrival and that the bears had not yet broken away *from* the areas of deep cover around their dens. In the afternoon we would ride back to camp, having seen many moose and wolf tracks, but no new sign of bear. You would sit hunched in the saddle at such times, your knees aching from all the riding, and listen to the wind in the tops of the tall jack pines. Everywhere in the dense timber, snags were blown over against standing trees; and where they crossed, the bark would be gone from each, and as they swayed together it would be like a wooden bow on a wooden string, producing notes of varied high keening pitches throughout the forest. In the cold air with the warm smell of the horse and saddle leather rising up to you, you'd listen to that music and wonder why you were never going to be able to figure grizzlies out.

Ray and I would invariably eat dinner—maybe bannock hot from the frying pan (the surest way to an Indian brave's heart), and chili with lots of fresh garlic—sitting at our lookout, glassing for bear. Ray'd have his .358 Winchester, and I my .375. I'd talk about Africa and Alaska; he'd talk about Tuchodi and goats to the north; how he'd won the guides association's championship buckle for grizzly his very first year out; and how the only backup some old-time outfitters would deign to carry when they were leading a client after grizzly was an *ax*.

" 'Just smack him *real* good between the eyes when he closes with you,' " Ray would quote these certifiable loons as explaining, all the while sweeping the country with his binoculars, the river below us looking molten in the sunset.

On the tenth day of the hunt I crawled out of my tent on all fours and stood up to see that someone had hung a mirror on a tree. I approached it with grave doubts. I had taken to wearing my coat of brown Pendleton wool constantly, and at night I was sleeping on spruce boughs like those that bears lined their dens with. I seemed to be walking with my back humped a great deal of the time. I'd pulled up a spring beauty one day just to sample the root, and the red kinnikinnick berries were beginning to look downright mouthwatering. More than once I found myself wondering which brand of beer went well with winter-killed moose, and if a snowslide wouldn't be a jolly thing to frolic in. Now I squinted at my reflection in the mirror and was not entirely surprised to note how grizzled my beard was becoming from the sun. It was obvious I was getting much too far *into* this business of bear.

That morning the Beatton was low enough for the first time in the hunt for us to ford it—our feet up on the horses' withers and our rifles drawn out of the scabbards—and hunt the other side. We rode up from the river to an old dirt road and there in the hardened mud was a track, not *brand*-spanking-new, certainly, but of a huge bear, a nine-footer or better. We got down and looked at it, then just stared at each other.

We rode off into the timber and found another track of a *different* bear, a little smaller paw print, but at most only hours old, leading up into some impenetrable cover. Then down along another nameless creek we found more tracks wandering over the sandbars. The bears, at last, were breaking loose, and we waited on a hill above the creek throughout the afternoon, waiting to see if anything would go up or down it in front of us. Finally we had to saddle up and ride back down to the Beatton, where we dismounted and jumped the horses off a high bank into the river—nostrils flaring, mud splattering—and reforded the fast water. We rode on into what Ray called "First Camp," a well-used cabin in a yellow meadow by a beaver pond where a field-guide's-worth of waterfowl, including six long-necked swans, paddled. We pulled our rifles from the scabbards, loosened the main lines on the saddles, and turned the horses out to graze on the green grass sprouting up through the dead yellow. As Ray and I sat among some beaver-felled poplars, eating peaches from a tin can, I thought of the bears on the other side of the river and tried to send word to them in my mind: Come across, you big-assed bears, come across. There is new fresh grass and tender roots over here. Come across.

And that night, back at our camp above the Beatton, when in my sleep I thought I heard the horses nickering nervously, or maybe in the first real light before I got out to the lookout to glass, or maybe while Ray and Mickey and I ate French toast and drank black coffee around the campfire at eight, one came across.

Ray turned the horses loose after breakfast to let them graze down the hill to the meadow. An hour and a half later he walked down, with his long loping stride, unconsciously checking around him for likely trees to shinny up should the need arise, to fetch them back up. The next time I saw Ray I was sitting on a log, trying one more time to read the *Iliad,* and he was galloping up the hill bareback on Shorty, the horse's black mane bunched in his white-knuckled fist. Ray was foaming. I got my rifle and followed him back down.

The bear had crossed somewhere upriver and come around the soft muddy bank, where the river made a bend, to the edge of the heavy timber walling off the far side of the meadow. Then he had gotten onto the wide bear trail and left his heavy, wide, long, fat-toed, big-assed, *grizzly* tracks for three hundred yards along it across the open meadow. He followed the trail on through the poplars before passing a hundred and fifty yards below our camp on the hill. If he scented us—and he had to down there where our tracks cut his trail, making him stare up our way with his myopic eyes—he never quickened his pace, but continued on up the canyon of the nameless creek. He was an old bear with many years in this country, with probably many encounters with men. He always let them go their way, while he went his. This trail was his.

An outdoor writer of some note, and wide experience with bears, once put the odds on spotting a grizzly during a fifteen-day hunt in the north country at roughly fifty-fifty, and it looked uncomfortably as if we'd just had our fifty. We did not follow the bear that day, fearful of running him out of the area, but let him go on upstream and hoped he'd discover some place to settle in and root to his heart's content. We rode after him the next day, trailing him until his track played out in a thicket of young willows. We spiraled around the country, then, seeking him, finding signs of more bears everywhere—but never the bears themselves—hearing the wind and wondering if it might be wolves. We stayed on past the fourteen days, till all our food and the horses' grain were gone. We broke camp then and hung the panniers from the pack saddles with basket hitches, threw the diamonds over the soft loads on top, tightened the cinches on our riding stock, and headed out. Back along the trail, we rode down to the Beatton and saw our first strangers—workmen loading clean gravel into the backs of trucks with a skip loader. We had to cross a bridge to get to where we'd parked the stock truck; and leading the now well-tried pack mare and not pausing to think, I rode old Shorty—old, reliable, steadfast, plodding Shorty with his hooves the size of soup plates and a disposition like cool stone—directly onto the wooden planks of the open bridge forty feet above the river, let him take one look down, and brought my first grizzly bear hunt to a close (in literally its final hundred paces) by having the half-ton of horse beneath me blow up as sky-high as a dynamite factory struck by lightning.

After the rodeo concluded and we got the horses somehow across the bridge and loaded back onto the truck, I had time to think about grizzlies and the Pomo Indians again. They were correct, of course, to insist upon a certain degree of maturity in hunters of the grizzly. But merely because at thirty you might have a right to *hunt* the great bear, it did not necessarily follow that you had also earned the right to kill him yet. That was something that might take even more years, or perhaps could never be earned.

In North America are some of the world's greatest big-game animals, and the bears are in the forefront of them. I had hunted the bear of Kodiak, and black bear in California, Oregon, and Alaska, and if it were ever possible again, I would find an Inuit with a dog team and cross the frozen white Arctic Sea to hunt polar bear. The greatest big-game animal in North America, though, and the one, I could now see, who would draw me back to grizzly country again and again, till I could be twice the Pomos' age of majority, remained downriver somewhere, clawing at the earth, lifting his heavy head to catch a spring breeze bringing him smells of new grasses and berries and animal flesh before passing through his fur like the wind in a ripe field of grain.

Delta New Year

It was between Christmas and the first of January. Most years this is a time for planning which New Year's Eve party to pass out at or deciding whose house to crawl to the next day to watch the bowl games. This year, though, it would be a time for going into the Delta with Fred Fortier and his young son Freddy B. It would be a time for staying in Fred's cabin at his old hunting club in Oxberry Bayou, going after ducks with a farmer friend of his in flooded rice fields in the morning, hunting deer in the club's hardwood timber in the afternoon, and drinking some whiskey in front of the fire at night. It would, in short, be a time for ending the year *right* for a change.

We made the long drive south from Ripley to Grenada County

with the three of us in the cramped cab of Fred's small Jeep pickup—and with a sneak boat lashed to the roll cage and two big net bags of decoys, shotgun and rifle cases, shotgun and rifle *shells,* waders, duffels, sleeping bags, a portable tree stand, and ice chests piled high in the back. As we rolled across the Tallahatchie Bridge, the stars were cold and sharp in the black sky, and Muddy Waters was coming out *strong* on the tape deck—Fred, as we neared Oxberry, exuberantly yanking his duck call off the rearview mirror and accompanying Muddy's blues harmonica with it. When we arrived in camp late that night, we asked Mr. Jesse Buck, the camp cook, to be sure to awaken us at 4:30 A.M., but as a precaution I set my alarm clock before turning in. I needn't have bothered.

Mr. Buck's fist hit the cabin door and he called out, "It is *exactly* four-thirty! You want one egg or *two?*" at the precise moment my alarm sounded the next morning. Ten minutes later we were in the brightly lit kitchen of the camp's main bunkhouse, eating eggs and bacon and corn bread and drinking hot coffee. Fred had warned me ahead of time that there had been so little rain in the fall, he had serious doubts whether there was a wet pothole to be found anywhere in all the counties of Grenada, Tallahatchie, Leflore, Sunflower, and Bolivar put together. But Bob Harris's rice fields had some water in them and we might just find a greenhead or two there.

It was still dark when we entered the Delta at the edge of Bob Harris's land, the line of demarcation between hill country and flatland being a gently sloping ridge, like a low dune at the rim of a great calm lake of soil. I was riding up in Bob Harris's pickup, and as we came over the ridge and the headlights streamed out into the predawn darkness where there was nothing rising up anymore to catch them, Bob said to me, "Well, you have just come into the Delta." And so I had.

We separated from Fred and Freddy B. there and drove around on the levees to one of the far fields near a brake of tall willow trees. Unloading the sack of dekes, Bob let me out, then reversed the truck several hundred yards back up the levee and out of sight, the lights going out like birthday candles. As he came walking back in the twilight, I could hear the flapping sound his rubber chest waders made long before I could see him again.

The water reached to our calves as we waded out into it, breaking through the skim ice and trying to stay out of the softest spots in the muddy bottom. Fred had been wrong; there was at least *one* wet pothole in the Delta, and when we reached it in the middle of the rice field, we tossed our dekes out.

"What we really ought to have are a couple of those little layout boats to lie in," Bob said with a shrug, then nonchalantly kicked out a place for himself in the ice and sat down. I glanced hopefully around for a dry spot, but, not finding one, sat down beside him in the mud, the frigid water washing up around my hips.

The dawn was beginning to seep across the surface of the pothole when the first black shape of a greenhead set into the spread, breaking the pink glassiness of the water. From my sitting position I tried to swing on him. He rose straight up and swept himself into the receding band of night to the west as I fired. All I could see then was an afterimage of the red flame; all I could hear was the duck's wings carrying him off into the dark.

As the sun climbed, it seemed only to grow colder as we sat in the wet field. Skeins of ducks would wheel and pass high above; but not even Bob's calling could bring them down to us, and they would disappear noisily behind the willow trees. Looking around, we saw ducks setting into a field at the opposite end of the rice land. You cannot make a duck land where he does not wish to, so we got up and collected the dekes and headed for the truck.

Now the cold really hit me and I began to shiver till it felt my bones would crack. My gloves were wet and the stock of my shotgun was splattered with mud. We climbed into the truck without pulling off our waders, smearing the gray Delta gumbo on the seat, and followed the levee around to the other field, the heater in the cab adjusted to "Equatorial" the entire way.

Fred and Freddy B. had one pintail between them when we waved them over. We set out all our dekes in the water by the levee and made blinds for ourselves in the levee's tall weeds. After a morning of sitting in what was more *ice* than water, to have dry weeds on a firm dirt bank to lie in while a yellow winter sun poured down on me was like being offered a scepter and a crown. Then the ducks came.

How many flights did Bob and Fred call in? Three? Four? Five? All I know is that, lying there with my shotgun drawn up beside me and the weeds pulled over me, I would peek out from under the brim of my camouflaged hat and see the mallards swinging by overhead. With each swing they would pass lower, until I could hear their *whoosh* as they came by.

"Next time," Fred would whisper around his *blues* duck call clenched in his teeth. Then he'd start blowing on it again, making all the metal leg bands on the lanyard chime.

They would come in from the east, crossing in front of us. You could see their colors brightly when they were this close. We would let them touch the water in the midst of the dekes before rising up.

"Only drakes now," Fred would call as the ducks flared, and I would lock onto a greenhead and fire, watching the big bird fold up and fall with his orange feet pedaling and his glossy-feathered head thrown back. I would wade out then to where he lay. As I hefted his warm body and watched the beads of water roll off his belly, I would turn and see Fred smiling out at me from the woods. I could see in his blue eyes, though—eyes as cold blue as a wolf's above a bushy buffalo hunter's mustache—that killing the ducks was the least of it for him. For Fred, calling those birds down from the sky was everything. The rest was only aftermath.

Late that afternoon, while Mr. Buck was cleaning our birds for the munificent sum of fifty cents apiece, Fred took me into the hardwoods. I had my .45-70 slung over my shoulder as I followed him between the trees. Fred halted and knelt down to look at a deer trail. He pointed out a tree and said for me to make my stand there. Then he disappeared, his portable tree stand on his back and his '06 held in his right hand.

I sat at the base of that tree that afternoon, watching the light leave the timber, listening to a dog running somewhere, thinking: There certainly are a number of different things you can do between Christmas and New Year's. You can always stay in a city somewhere and go to too many parties and drink too much with people who are never going to have the slightest understanding of what it is you *do* with your life, or of how *hunting* could possibly mean so much to you that you would gladly travel halfway across a continent just to spend a day or two with one of the few of your friends who understands *perfectly*. Or you could spend it as I now was, hunting hard all day *with* that friend and going to bed early in a piney-smelling cabin in a silent forest in order to be up early the next morning to go at it again. Sitting there, I could only hope that next year was going to turn out one-tenth as well as this one was ending.

At last light I heard Fred fire once. Standing, I slung my .45-70 back over my shoulder. I started toward where the shot had come from, then heard Fred call out. I met him dragging a fat, sleek whitetail doe over the fallen leaves.

We would be going a little farther afield tomorrow, trying to pack as much into the waning year as we could. When we returned to camp and got the deer hung up, we asked Mr. Buck to wake us in the morning at four. This time I didn't worry about clocks.

Goin' 'Gatorin'

The night is warm. As the dog climbs out from his nest of burlap sacks beneath the double-wide mobile home, there is the din of crickets and bullfrogs in the air, air as heavy as damp wool. The dog is a Doberman pinscher—some eighty pounds or better of Doberman pinscher, in fact, all muscle and pointed alert ears and a mouthful of white teeth. He bows his sleek back and stretches gracefully, then turns and watches the traffic go by on Highway 90. The dog turns back and smells the canal. He pads down to the water's edge a few yards behind the aluminum trailer. He stands there a moment, his ears especially high, then warily lowers his muzzle to drink. A quiet ripple in the water lilies floating over the canal's surface makes him snap his head up, the metal tags on his chain collar jangling. He stands poised, listening. A minute passes. When no more sound comes from the canal, the dog goes back to drinking.

The eleven-foot bull alligator breaks the water in a rush, and before the dog can leap away, the many round conical teeth of this reptile, our last living link to the dinosaur, close on the Doberman's neck. The 'gator pulls the struggling dog back into the canal and begins to spin his own heavy long body along its vertical axis, churning gray mud up from the shallow bottom. When he stops, the dog in his jaws no longer struggles. The mud begins to settle back to the bottom as the cars go on by on Highway 90.

Once millions of alligators swam and slithered and floated and rolled and roared and lay absolutely motionless, basking on the dry ridges, or chéniers, in the swamps of Louisiana and the rest of the South, and nobody quite knew what to make of them all. The Spaniard named the alligators he encountered during his explorations of subtropical North America *el lagarto,* "the lizard," but the alligator is of an order much different from the lizard, belonging to that group of reptiles known as the Archosauria, or "ruling reptiles" (which included the dinosaurs). They appeared on earth some 180 to 160 million years ago, during the Triassic geological period. Today they are the closest living relative of the *bird.*

In the mid-1770s, the artist, traveler, and naturalist William Bartram—the son of John Bartram, called the world's greatest natural botanist by none other than Linnaeus, and the "father of American botany" by any number of others—made an extended exploratory expedition through Florida and up the St. Johns River. At one point in his travels, his Indian companion abandoned him in a "fine orange grove," but he pressed on alone. Traveling in his small boat, he encountered the then ubiquitous and aggressive reptile in a most vivid fashion as he beheld an alligator "rushing forth from the flags and reeds. His enormous body swells. His plaited tail brandished high, floats upon the lake. The waters like a cataract descend from his opening jaws. Clouds of smoke issue from his nostrils. The earth trembles with his thunder." (Bartram's *Travels,* it is not surprising, were greatly admired by the English Romantic poets, particularly Coleridge.)

Farther on, Bartram was forced to cudgel his way past bold 'gators as he paddled out to fish in a lagoon, the reptiles trying to capsize his tiny barque. Back on the islet where he was making a camp, he was nearly caught like a dog in one of the "subtle attacks" of an alligator as he was cleaning his catch, and had the beast sweep a number of the fish into the water with his tail. Another 'gator who persisted in crawling up onto the shore and threatening him Bartram had to dispatch "by lodging the contents of my gun into his head." Later that day he saw the river blocked from bank to bank by shoals of migrating fish, and the alligators feeding on them were in "such incredible numbers" and packed so tightly together that one might have stepped across the wide river on their heads, "had the animals been harmless." The 'gators consumed hundreds of thousands of fish, the noise of their eating frenzy keeping Bartram awake well into the night.

Bartram is said to have reported seeing alligators twenty feet long, and John James Audubon to have killed a seventeen-footer. A figure that is reported in several reputable locales lists nineteen feet two inches as the official mark set by one Louisiana 'gator. Maybe so. Maybe such an alligator could have been disproportionately long and serpentile, or if he was of characteristic build he must have weighed a ton. And where would such a brute abide, and upon what would he feed? (Thirteen or fourteen feet is widely regarded as a kind of reasonable maximum to expect any 'gator in the wild to reach nowadays—though who's to say what could be lurking up some bayou somewhere?)

The alligator continued relatively unmolested well into the nineteenth century. His mild firm meat supported many of the settlements of the water-logged South through their lean and formative years, and that was about all he had to contend with. He was even transformed into part of the frontier's mythology as the Kentucky keelboatmen who would steer their cargoes of tobacco and livestock down the mighty Mississip' to New Orleans boasted lavishly of being "alligator-horses"—half-horse, half-alligator centaurs—whose main purpose in life seemed to be, after unloading their vessels, to do as much gambling, drinking, dueling, and general all-around *roaring* as was humanly—or *in*humanly—possible.

Then in 1855 the fashion designers of Paris decreed alligator leather to be the latest trend, and a market for the hides opened. To this was soon coupled the Civil War's need for additional sources of durable leather. Pressure on the reptiles grew. E. A. McIlhenny of Avery Island, Louisiana (and Tabasco Brand Pepper Sauce fame), estimated that 3 million alligators were killed in the state between 1880 and 1933, and state tax records indicate another 314,404 were taken legally between 1939 and 1955. Wetlands drainage, depriving the 'gators of both room and board, had also been added along the way to the soup the reptiles were finding themselves increasingly in, and by the late 1950s their numbers had reached such a low point in Louisiana that it seemed no one would care to venture a guess as to how *few* there might be left.

Then in 1958 the state initiated an alligator research program. It followed this in 1960 by passing laws to establish a closed season and size limit on 'gators. In 1963 the entire state was closed to all alligator hunting. On Rockefeller Refuge near Grand Chenier in Louisiana a radio-collaring program was begun on alligators in 1969. In that same year the Lacey Act was amended to control the interstate commerce in reptile hides. The alligator was later included in the Endangered Species Act and the CITES Treaty and soon began making his return.

By the mid-1960s his return was such that it had become obvious that live capture and transplanting of 'gators to new areas was not keeping pace with the population rise, so 1972 saw the first legal alligator hunt in Louisiana in almost ten years, the hunt being considered the most legitimate way of dealing with the surplus of the animals. Then 1975 saw the alligator reclassified as "threatened by similarity of appearance" in several parishes in Louisiana, with many more parishes added in a few short years. The illicit market was virtually eliminated—alligators are now among the most stringently regulated animals around, to the extent that even special skinning instructions are issued just days before each season opens to prevent poachers from affixing a tag to an out-of-season 'gator and slipping it into the legal trade—and nonresidents were again permitted to hunt the Louisiana alligator.

The Louisiana population now stands at some 600,000, and the species has demonstrated the potential for an average annual increase of 55.5 percent. The 'gator population of greater New

Orleans *alone* is said to stand at one per every thirty citizens. According to the late epicurean writer Waverly Root, in a piece on the reptile as table fare, alligators have taken to showing up on golf courses, lawn parties, and church services, to the consternation of everyone concerned. They have taken to eating Dobermans. More than 16,000 alligator tags were issued in Louisiana in 1982. I had one of them.

The late afternoon was hot and the sweat had spread in a blotch of cool darkness across the back of my shirt. We were in guide Pete Duran's aluminum boat on a canal in a place known as the Pleasure Ponds, near where Dobermans and other dogs, as well as ducks and chickens and *God* knows what else, had been eaten, in the area of Lac des Allemands. It was early September, the day before Louisiana's alligator season was scheduled to open, and we were setting baits.

Bait for an alligator consists of a two-pound mullet—which attains superior quality after it has hung out for two or three days and has had the smell of human hands supplanted by something a bit more robust—on a No. 3 shark hook, dangling a foot or so above the murky water (to prevent turtles and undersize 'gators from reaching it). The hook is attached to a goodly length of No. 96 rot-resistant tarred 100 percent nylon seine twine, with a tensile strength of 911 pounds, set in the notched end of an ash pole, called a *picket,* with the other end tied off to a real strong tree firmly rooted in a canal bank.

I was pushing the sharpened end of a picket into the muddy canal bottom while Pete tied the twine's end off around the base of the tree. My father, who had come hunting with me, was placing the hook in the body of a dead mullet so the fish was bent up like the letter *U*. Hooking dead mullet for 'gator bait was a newly acquired talent for him, but one that after only a few fish he had learned to perform with some expertise. He examined his work and was justly satisfied. Pete set the line in the picket's notch and adjusted the bait's height. Leaning back, he appraised the display, deciding how it would appeal to an alligator.

"*Bon,*" he said finally. He fired up the hundredfold-horsepower motor of his flat-bottomed fishing boat, and we went skimming out of the canal into the smooth, sunstruck open water of the ponds, heading to place another of the thirty or forty baits we would need for the next day. Pete drove the boat standing up in the stern. He wore blue denims and a white T-shirt over his round belly, a tall, tall straw hat set squarely on his head of thick, black hair, and white rubber boots on his feet, lending him the air of a lunar explorer. Pete was Cajun.

Parsing out the noun *Cajun* can be no mean feat. To begin with, you have to go back to Arcadia, a mountainous, backwoods sort of district of southern Greece's Peloponnesus. Probably because they didn't know a thing about it except its lyric name, classical Greek and Latin poets selected Arcadia to be, in the words of the Oxford English Dictionary, "the ideal region of rural contentment." Now jump forward from B.C. to the middle of the second millennium A.D., and as William Faulkner Rushton outlines in his book *The Cajuns,* you have the explorer Verrazano, mindful of his classics, slapping the name on a landfall in southern North America. The name heads north with succeeding maps until it comes to rest on Nova Scotia, where the local Indians have a similar-sounding word, *Akade,* for a similar concept of heaven on earth. Thus we arrive at the word *Acadia.*

The French, primarily Celts from Brittany who have been fishing on the Grand Banks off Newfoundland since the beginning of the sixteenth century, settle Acadia, in time making it a crown colony of France. But the English gain control over most of that colony in 1713; then in 1755, following many years of political unrest, they expel five thousand Acadians from Nova Scotia. The Acadians' diaspora, complicated by the Seven Years' War, goes on for some time, until a number of them reach Louisiana. Here English-speaking Americans mangle their name into "Cajuns"—the same way Indians became "Injuns," and with a show of about as much respect. And all of the above cannot even *begin* to explain Cajuns.

A Cajun is proud of his name, though. He even seems to enjoy his other, looser cognomen of "coon-ass." There appears to be no connection between this name and those hardy members of the Procyonidae the raccoons. The name, in fact, is believed by eminent linguists to be from an archaic French profanation (the French having a word for *everything*) *"conasse,"* which to my understanding means, more or less, that is to say, er . . . a poxy whore. It is always good policy, à la Owen Wister's *The Virginian,* to *smile* when you call someone a Cajun. It is downright *essential* when you call him a *coonass*.

We began hunting 'gators at first light of opening morning. In the olden days you could also legally hunt 'gators at night, and in many ways night hunting was a more exciting venture. You would idle over the water in the soft buzzing darkness, wearing a miner's head lamp and carrying a six-volt battery in your back pocket. When you picked out a pair of eyes burning bright as brake lights in a nighttime rush hour, you could, with sufficient skill, use a .22 short and, taking aim along an angle 30 degrees or so off the midline of the reptile's head, fire a bullet through the eye and down a septum leading through the casemate of his skull and directly into the brain—a brain, by the way, and I have seen this without quite believing it, just about the size of the final joint on the tip of your little finger. That, apparently, is all the cerebral matter needed to command up to a dozen feet and a quarter-ton of, let's face it, *dinosaur*. All it takes to get him to lay his stubby legs back along his body and send him torpedoing through the water with powerful, lateral, wavelike motions of his tail. But if you managed to hit it he would die instantly.

Another unique aspect of night hunting was the opportunity it afforded for gliding up from behind on foot-long yearlings and snatching them up just in back of their necks and lifting them out of the water. 'Gators of this age and size were as cute as a minute, cool and green and yelping like puppies. A hunter could hold one up in the light and coo at him and burble until the hunter would bring him too close and the little sucker'd clamp ahold of his upper lip for dear life.

The 'gator hunting season in Louisiana is set well after the alligators' time of breeding, to help protect the population even further. This goal is what is behind the outlawing of another colorful hunting technique known as poling. This involved following a female's wide trail across a chénier to her den. A long pole was then shoved into the den and swizzled around until mama 'gator came roaring out, gnawing on the pole's end. While she was engaged in reducing the pole to matchsticks, somebody'd smack her real good on the head with the back of a hatchet and then lug her out to the bayou, leaving the eggs or hatchlings to fend for themselves.

That opening morning, the first baited line we checked had a 'gator on it, lying, unmoving, back up on a weedy bank, glaring out at us with its cat eyes. We looked at it, decided it was not big enough, and cut it free, Pete having to climb out onto the bank to cut the twine, and having to leap back into the boat as the 'gator charged toward him to get back into the water. We moved on to check the other baits.

Anyone with hopes of shooting an alligator swimming on the water, or lying sunning on a bank, I soon saw, should quickly disabuse himself of them. I assure you, any basking 'gator worth his salt will hit the water with great swiftness at the first sight or sound of an approaching boat. And the best target a swimming 'gator is likely to present is just his eyes and nostrils showing above the waterline at absolutely no less than a hundred and fifty yards. This means you would get to attempt a shot, from a bobbing boat, at the flat surface of a bayou, at a kill spot the size of your fist, *underneath* the surface, on a prehistoric animal which, if your bullet didn't ricochet off to God knows where, or didn't merely *wound* the reptile (and a couple of inches either way is all it takes to turn a good shot into a bad one on a 'gator), which if it actually *did* succeed in killing him outright, would be apt to send the alligator straight to the bottom, however deep it might be—in short, dead 'gators don't float.

After the day's first 'gator had been turned loose, we went up the long canal leading from the Pleasure Ponds to Lac des Allemands itself. The open water was choppy as we went banging over it at planing speed. Most of the baits were still hanging along the shore where the big cypresses grew, though some had been pulled down by the drifting banks of water lilies or by the efforts of herons. Then we saw a 'gator lying blackly on the shore, the heavy brown line running from his closed jaws. Seeing us, he slid with great swiftness into the water. We pulled him up again, but a foot or so of his tail had been lost to history or experience, and we let him go too.

Our round of bait checking sent us back to the Pleasure Ponds, where we pulled up one downed line and found it had a blue cat of no less than fifty pounds attached to it. We killed the fish and brought him aboard for the camp's dinner. Then we went off to check our last bait, this one near where dogs kept getting gobbled by something very large.

'Gator "hunting" is really an amalgam of the three disciplines of hunting, trapping, and fishing. What it vaguely resembles is the running of an extended trotline, over an area of many, many square miles, for wet things with big teeth. Yet it can be best understood only for what it uniquely is: *'gatorin',* an undertaking not exactly like anything else. The techniques of 'gatorin' for sport are pretty much the same long-used techniques of commercial alligator hunting (the sport permit even comes stamped on a trapper's license). At its least interesting, 'gatorin' is about like shooting a rather large, exquisitely crafted, exotic Louis Vuitton leather suitcase. At its *most* interesting, however, it can remind its warm-blooded participants of nothing so much as all the mobilized Defense Forces of Japan battling to halt some rubber-suit monster in its tracks as it slouches toward a scale model of the Ginza, bursting high-tension wires and flattening streetcars en route.

When we came to that last bait that morning, it was the turn of a bow hunter to see what Pete would find at the end of the line, if anything. When Pete nosed the boat up to the bank, the line was slanting tautly down into a hole under it. Pete grabbed the line and tugged. The line tugged back, violently, and the fight was on. When Pete finally got the 'gator's head up, the mightiest set of toothed jaws I had ever seen appeared above the surface, swamp water cascading out of them. I shuddered involuntarily. The bowman was ready, leaning over the gunwale, his 65-pound compound drawn back and the broadhead aimed for the tiny kill spot just behind the thick boiler plate of the alligator's skull and in front of the broad shield of bony buckles mailing his back. And when he fired, he almost hit it. But when the arrow, instead of penetrating, bounced off the 'gator's head, the big bull simply went berserk, rolling and thrashing until he threw the hook.

He took off then up the canal just like leviathan from the Book of Job—for whom, as it was spoken out of the whirlwind, "darts are counted as stubble"—making a "path to shine after him" as he marked his progress along the soft bottom with a trail of silvery sulfurous bubbles. Then the bubbles stopped, the 'gator lying on the bottom, waiting for us to go away. He had no gills, only lungs, and he was holding his breath. We floated over him, waiting silently. The heat was windless and fierce. An immense bank of water lilies, green flecked with purple, drifted slowly by us on the current.

One hour and fifteen minutes after the alligator had gone down, he surfaced. The bowman now fired a pistol shot at him, grazing his head. The alligator swam out of the canal and into the shallow open water of the Pleasure Ponds, Pete and the bowman following in one boat, and the rest of us in another. Pete overtook the 'gator in the pond, and this time when the reptile raised his head, the hunter put a bullet into it. Pete grabbed the animal's tail and one webbed, clawed foot and hollered for us to get over to him before the 'gator sank. We came aboard Pete's boat like a party of privateers seizing His Majesty's flagship, and each of us grabbed ahold of a section of alligator. I had the tail now, black as a truncheon and big around as a man's waist.

What if this billion-year-old bastard's undead? I wondered. What if he's merely stunned or playing possum and should come to with a start, slamming his two hundred pounds of tail muscle around inside this aluminum boat? Do I abandon ship and hope he stays on board, or do I try to stay on board and hope he somehow flails himself out without me clamped in his jaws? I couldn't figure what the answer was, so I just kept pulling. We got all of him in, and while the hunter was attaching his yellow plastic tag to the tail, Pete methodically bound the jaws shut with seine twine, just to be on the safe side.

Back at camp we hung this monster-of-the-day up before skinning him. He was an 11½-foot bull—females seldom get over nine foot—and an honest 400 pounds or better in weight. After we skinned and filleted him, one of our party, a physician, had an idea. The good doctor was an inveterate prober and examiner, and he was curious to know what might be on the inside of this alligator. I, for some reason I have yet to understand, volunteered to assist him in the operation, but when we opened up the 'gator's stomach, the smell was far beyond my dizziest imaginings. The doc, however, was in his element. When he could not ascertain to his satisfaction visually what the 'gator had been dining on, he thought nothing of plunging his hand inside the cavity. He proceeded to remove bunches of water lily leaves. Large chunks of acid-etched driftwood. Turtle shells. Whitened alligator tails. Unspeakable muck. Plastic shotgun hulls. And, finally, as the pièce de résistance, two empty two-liter, clear plastic soft-drink bottles. Obviously, there was no such thing as foreign matter to an alligator's alimentary canal, but even as I was trying to keep from retching, I was somewhat disappointed that no partially digested choke chains had been found along with everything else.

I killed a good 'gator of nearly eight feet a few mornings later. The kill was one shot and clean, a 405-grain .45-70 doing the job. I spent the afternoon helping to skin him out. The belly and flank leather was supple and strong, pebbly-grained and pleasant to look at. I would have the hide tanned and stretch it across the wall of my living room to remind me, when the weather turned cold, of Louisiana September days.

We filleted off all the good meat, careful to remove as much of the fat from it as we possibly could. That evening in the air-conditioned hunting cabin, with my father and the other hunters gathered there pleased as well with the 'gators they had all taken, Dub Martin, Pete Duran's fishing partner, 'gator guide, and camp cook par excellence, prepared a genuine Cajun alligator sauce piquante for us from the meat of my kill. When served, it proved delicious, somewhere between veal and pork in flavor. Through the cabin window as I ate I saw, framed by Spanish moss hanging from Spanish oaks, great blue herons sailing across a cinnabar sunset. 'Gators and birds, huh?

Would I be back to do this again? I asked myself. I couldn't say. All I knew was that I was glad to have been here once.

Days on the Water

Five rivers and arroyos, the San Carlos, Pilón, Purificación, Corona, and El Charón, were once splayed fingers leading to the Río Soto la Marina and the sea. In this 79,829-square-kilometer state of Tamaulipas—whose northern boundary is a panhandle of land lying along the Río Bravo with Texas on the other bank, the land then widening and turning south to fill the region between Atlantic water and the Sierra Madre Oriental, which is known as the Sierra Gorda locally and which reaches to over 13,000 feet at its highest peaks—these rivers in the past drained the center of the Gulf Coastal Plain of Mexico. Now in this temperate mesquite and grassland country just this side of the tropic, there is a lake where no lake stood before.

Over 100,000 acres of land are covered by the dammed-up waters of Lake Vicente Guerrero, supplying 5 billion cubic meters of water annually for modern practices of irrigation. Back in the year and month of my birth, some twenty years before the lake, A. Starker Leopold surveyed the waterfowl of this Soto la Marina River system and found neither blue-winged teal nor green-winged, gadwall, shoveler, canvasback, nor pintail. Thirty-one years later in a late February, I went to a lodge on the lake to hunt these ducks, which, along with widgeon and cinnamon teal and other species, the water now draws there in great number.

When I first meet the *patrón* of the lodge—a moneyed Texan who keeps a Mexican partner somewhere—he is wearing a safari hat and standing at a fourteen-inch band saw in the woodshop he has had constructed behind his large apartment at the lodge, roughing out the form of a teal from two blocks of sugar pine bolted together. As he works he tells me how he had always wanted to hunt over a set of decoys handmade by himself and one morning the previous spring had arisen and taken up a chunk of wood in one hand and a paring knife in the other and set out to carve a duck. An hour later he had produced little more than a blister big as a fair-size walnut and decided he was going to have to learn *really* how a duck was carved.

"Fourteen thousand dollars later," he says, not making a long story merely short, but positively truncated, "I was in the decoy business." He pulls the wood away from the blade and eyeballs the line of the belly, then puts it to the blade again, sawdust floating into the air. He can now carve ducks of extreme detail and not a small amount of grace. Besides turning out his decoys, he has built a sprawling lodge on raw scrub land on the lake's shore, has hunted and fished and scuba-dived intensively himself throughout the world, and goes so far as to keep bobcats and mountain lions as house pets. He is a man who takes his whims seriously.

The first morning on the lake is cold enough for a wool sweater. The afternoon before, after my arrival, I shot with the *patrón* in the drowned mesquite timber up the flooded Río Pilón, and the shade had been welcome. The shooting was slow and I sat on a low dead limb, my feet floating in my waders on the muddy water as I listened sleepily to the warm wind in the high tules around me, rattling them like sabers. Now as the guide Rogelio runs by sheer memory across the predawn lake to the Río Purificación, the wind has a bite to it that keeps me wide awake.

There are Rogelio and I in our boat this morning, with two other Mexicans, one another guide and the other there to help set out the decoys and beat the swamp to stir up the birds for me, in a second boat. We ride until there is not enough water for the boats' drafts, then get out and wade through soft mud into a shallow lagoon hidden by tules. There is a blind there made of dead moss draped around some old snags with a bare wooden bench placed inside for a seat. As the Mexicans set out the decoys, I can see ducks lifting up far out across the low dead trees. Then the Mexicans are gone, and I wait quietly.

When I hear the Mexicans again, they are hooting and cursing at the ducks as they wade around me at a far perimeter. One of the guides has stayed with the boats and beats the side of his as he shouts. Then the ducks are flying. I crouch as they come toward the blind, and rise up as they start to set into the decoys. The Mexican No. 6 shells bang hard in the 870 and the ducks, mostly shovelers and teal, begin to drop. I shoot fast for two hours until it becomes too warm for a sweater, then the gray-haired Mexican who is not a guide comes to collect me. He is wearing chest waders smeared with dry gray mud, and when he sees the ducks I have taken he is pleased. He strings them together with a length of twine and counts out loud in Spanish, using a piece of stick to draw the number for me on the back of his hand when he is done, the numerals showing momentarily white on his brown skin before fading. I have killed a dozen or so, and that is enough for this morning.

Before the afternoon hunt we run on the lake down past the Río Purificación. Then we come back to the shallow water and I wade in to the same seat again, smelling the sulfur my feet suck up from the bottom. As I approach the blind, I see ducks getting up from the set; and as I am coming out from behind some tall trees, a blue-winged teal is flying low at me. I crouch and jack a green plastic shell into the chamber, and when I stand and fire, the duck tumbles almost to my feet.

The afternoon brings in fewer birds and is in a way more pleasant. There are more pintails and widgeon this afternoon, and as I look out across the dead scrub trees, the trunks banded black by the old high-water mark and the bare branches above bleached white as bones, I have time to watch the ducks come slipping their way through, wheeling and banking without touching a twig. When the gray-haired Mexican comes for me at dusk, he again counts the ducks, now fewer, and because I know Spanish, though badly, asks if I will be speaking with the *patrón* this evening.

I tell him yes, and the Mexican asks me please to say to him that he, the Mexican, says the *patrón* is a great man. I promise, wondering exactly what the hell *century* it is I'm in here.

The name Tamaulipas is said to derive anciently from a Huastec word, *Tamalihopa,* meaning "Place of the Olives," a tribe of the southern region of the state. The Huastecs were a Mayan-speaking coastal people considered to possess the highest degree of cultural development among the aboriginal tribes inhabiting Tamaulipas. They were mound builders and growers of cotton, but confined themselves primarily to the basin of the Guayalejo-Tamesi River in the south. The interior of the state, which for the first two centuries of their occupation of Mexico the Spanish found too desolate even to contemplate populating, was originally the territory of the nomadic Indians the Aztecs named the Chichimecs, meaning roughly "lineage of the dog." This was not the slander it might at first seem, since many of the rulers in the Valley of Mexico readily claimed Chichimec blood, perhaps in the same manner in which on St. Patrick's Day all politicians are Irish.

Still, the Chichimecs were thought a most barbarous lot by the Aztecs. They had a language shared by tribes possibly as far removed as California, and up into what is now Texas and Louisiana, but they insisted on painting their faces and bodies, wearing the skins of animals and sandals made of yucca fiber, and living in caves. With bows and arrows they hunted rabbits and peccary and deer and birds—nearly anything except roadrunners, which they protected because they fed on rattlesnakes. They speared and trapped fish on the rivers and gathered fruits and berries and roots and peyote from the "Hill of the Air," which would lead them to perform lengthy celebratory dances unaccompanied by any musical instruments other than the ones blowing rhythmically through their brain cells.

The Chichimecs were not an aggressive people, unless called upon to defend what they saw as their land. The Spanish, who knew that land simply as the coast of the Mexican Gulf, and later the province of Nuevo Santander, never encountered any hostility as they passed through it with their salt caravans en route to the Laguna Madre. The Chichimecs were represented by numerous tribes in the basin of the Río Purificación. One, at what is now the southern edge of the water of Lake Vicente Guerrero, was named *Los Ojos de la Tierra*, the Eyes of the Earth.

As we head into the lodge after sunset, I can feel the night hurrying toward me across the water from the east, the night a cool wind. We bounce heavily in the chop, and Rogelio now wields the beam of a 200,000-candlepower light over our bow to find a channel cut through the dead trees. Ducks and coots clatter away from us in the light as we run at them, and the branches of the trees twist up whitely out of the dark, the ghosts of trees.

That night in the lodge's trophy-hung "Safari Bar," I deliver the message to the *patrón* and eat filleted duck breasts that have been wrapped around white cheese and deep fried. Later I sit alone in the darkness on the second-story patio outside the bar and see Orion and a waxing moon, and listen to the cries of coyotes.

I go to hunt the same blind one more time the next morning. As we are running up to the place I will begin to wade from again, Rogelio catches in the light a big bull canvasback swimming. A live canvasback always looks to me more like a decoy of a canvasback, more like some of the *patrón*'s handiwork, than a decoy does, but my mind is actually elsewhere. Yesterday afternoon before going back out shooting we traveled down to the town of Old Padilla on the flooded bank of the Río Purificación. As we approached it, we saw the empty church on the lake shore and a long building with an archway running through its middle and ornamental turrets of pink stone topping the façade.

"*Mi escuela,*" Rogelio said with some pride.

The school was now some way out into Lake Vicente Guerrero and looked as if it had been cut adrift after being abandoned by all hands—the *Marie Celeste* of primary education. The water reached to the ledges of the glassless windows, but I had no way of knowing how much more might lie beneath the surface. Nothing else of Old Padilla showed above. I had never seen a town buried by water before.

The province of Nuevo Santander did not become the state of Tamaulipas until Mexico gained its independence from Spain. The Mexican War of Independence was a fitful uprising stretching over more than a decade from the "cry of Dolores" on September 16, 1810, until the Plan of Iguala, the Mexican Declaration of Independence, in 1821. During this time, various republican leaders came to the fore to achieve often spectacular, though short-lived, successes in the field, only eventually to have to meet the members of their firing squads at dawn.

It was not until a military coup brought a liberal government to Spain, and the church and gentry of Mexico came to fear the confiscation of their property, that Augustín de Iturbide, a royalist and former officer of the army of Spain responsible for suppressing many of the preceding revolutions, was able to unite the country's many factions and establish Mexico as a constitutional monarchy under a European prince, with a national congress and a junta of regents to which he was elected president. His presidency was predictably brief for a man of Iturbide's ambitions, however, and on July 21, 1822, at the age of thirty-eight, he was crowned the first Emperor of Mexico since Moctezuma's successor, Cuautémoc. The state of Tamaulipas was alone in voicing opposition to the coronation.

Iturbide's ascension, though, could not prevent the resurrection of republican sentiment. At the same time a wave of crime broke out in the newly freed nation. Iturbide reacted to these threats to his rule by muzzling the press and dissolving the congress. New revolutions sprang up, and he was forced to abdicate and go into European exile.

Not even a pension given him for life, however, could long persuade Iturbide not to return to Mexico to offer it his aid when he received word that Spain meant to invade his homeland. He sailed from England unaware that the new Mexican government had decreed him to be a traitor should he ever set foot in the country again. He landed on the coast north of Tampico in July of 1824 and, wearing a bandanna to mask his face, rode toward the town of Soto la Marina, near which he was, in spite of his disguise, recognized and arrested by troops of Tamaulipas' military commandant. Marched to the state's provisional capital in Padilla, where the state congress was in session, he put his case before them and was speedily ordered to be executed.

On July 19, having confessed his sins to a priest three times and having asked that the gold coins he carried in his pocket be paid to the riflemen after his execution, Iturbide knelt with bound arms in the plaza of Old Padilla and received the volley of shots. The site of the death of the former emperor, *El Libertador* of Mexico, as his tomb would read when his body was later moved to Mexico City, was marked for many years in Padilla by a monument, until in 1971 the water of Lake Vicente Guerrero reached to cover it.

The second morning at sunrise I make a triple on baldpates, the three ducks falling in a row, one after another. It is the end of the season, though, and the birds have grown decoy-shy. I kill a few more this morning and leave for a new place for the afternoon.

Going to the new blind built on a shore of deep green pasture where cattle graze, I wade carefully beside the wood posts of an old fence. Looking up, I see hundreds and hundreds of ducks rising from the grass where they have been feeding. They flare out over the distant dead scrub and begin to settle into the water beneath it.

In the blind of tules on the shore there is a crate for me to set my shell boxes on. It is very hot, and I roll my hip waders down around my calves in seven-league fashion to keep cool. The ducks come back over in ones and twos, and it is purely pass shooting this afternoon. They are all American widgeon, and when I kill a duck I immediately retrieve it and bring it into the blind to lay it on the wooden crate in the shade. When it is time to go, I have four or five of the white-headed birds lying on the box—more than enough to make a good day's hunting for me, or for anybody. Pulling up my waders, I head back out to the waiting boat with the sun going down behind the Sierra Gorda at my back. I see in the water ahead of me the moon reflected, while in the wake my feet leave the twilight glows.

The next morning is cool and gray. Before my plane leaves, I have time to take my bait-casting rod and go out with a fishing guide to try to catch some Florida bass, which the lake now produces in great plenty. We run for half an hour to where there is submerged structure and trees, and the *guía* attaches the clips from his electric trolling motor to a black car battery and begins to pull us around the shore of the lake with a soft whir.

Vicente Guerrero, for whom the lake is christened, was a young mixed-blood muleteer from the town of Tixtla near Acapulco. In the early days of the War of Independence his courage, his extensive knowledge of southern Mexico gained from his travels with his mule trains, and his fierce hatred of the *gachupines* ("the wearers of spurs," as the Spanish-born officials and landowners were contemptuously known) elevated him to the command of the revolution's southern front. Over the long course of the war, Guerrero remained an intractable guerrilla chieftain for the republican cause. Taking to the mountains when he had to, he overcame not only dysentery, an outbreak of smallpox among his troops, a bullet wound through both lungs, and military setbacks, but also a viceregal offer of a pardon and a governmental sinecure if he would only abandon his revolutionary activities. These he would never abandon.

After Iturbide, General Antonio López de Santa Anna (who had first gained battlefield experience as a young officer in the Spanish wars against the Huastecs in Tamaulipas, and who would rise up again and again to gain control of Mexico during the first thirty years of the republic) made the great warlord Guerrero the second president of Mexico in 1829, only to have him deposed and, on February 14, 1831, executed. In 1833 when Santa Anna took power as president in his own name for the first time, he declared Iturbide—whom he had also betrayed—a national hero and had his portrait hung in all of Mexico's public offices.

I fish a crank bait lure in Lake Vicente Guerrero. In two and a half hours I catch and release thirty bass, one a three-pounder, and have a big female twice that size up to the boat before she throws the hook. It is time to go then.

As we start back I ask the guide if there are any *tigres*— jaguar—around.

"*Sí*," he says, nodding with vigor. "*Y léones, y muchos venados,*" he adds, holding two fingers at each side of his head to mime "deer."

That would have been something, I think, to have been here in the days before the lake—although also before the ducks and the bass—and been able then to hunt *tigre* along one of the river canyons, waiting on a stand above a dead peccary, an Indian with Chichimec blood in him tugging the beeswaxed braided-horsehair cord of a *pujandero,* the jaguar call made from a gourd to imitate the grunting roar of a male *tigre,* as night fell.

I suppose it is only natural to think of past days, but those are not the days we now have. This lake, named for a dead muleteer and covering the place where an emperor died, has taken some things, I think, but left others in their place, and you live in the day you have in the best way you can.

As we make for the lodge and the plane, I see a hawk of a species I do not know swoop down onto the water and lift a coot off it. He carries it to the yellow rocks on the shore, where he kills it. As the raptor mantles his prey and begins to feed, he takes no notice of our passing.

The Fire in the Beast

When beasts went together in companies, there was said to be . . . a singular of boars, a sounder of wild swine, and a dryft of tame swine.
—JOSEPH STRUTT,
The Sports and Pastimes
of the People of England, 1838

What I *can* say is this: There is just something about the hunting of wild pigs.

The last April I hunted them in California was the coldest I had ever known. It was in the Chinese Year of the Boar, and the mornings in the Diablo Range of Monterey County brought the first hard freezes the ground had seen all season. As I worked down the grassy ridges before light, the bent blades would slough off heavy frost, wetting my boots through and leaving my feet aching. At night as I rode back down the old dirt roads in the open back of a pickup the black air would numb my hands as I gripped the steel rim of the truck box with one and held my empty rifle up with the other. A sign that it *was* spring, and not the heart of winter, was the afternoon hail that fell hard as rock salt, and the layers of white fat the boars were starting to put back on.

In such a cold time it seemed no more than the hand of fate that we would have a guide named August. We had been hunting with him for two days now on some of the 15,000 acres of land his father both owned and leased the hunting rights to. This land was rolling in parts and steep in others, with oak groves in the draws and hillsides variously open or choked with black sage, the hilltops peaked by stands of Digger pines. And despite the upside-down weather, the new barley had somehow managed to be already well up in the fields, as were the wild oats and the volunteer barley from the year before. On the ridges stood tall yellow wallflowers, too; and more deer and quail were to be seen than any law-abiding man should by rights be compelled to encounter out of season.

We had already killed a pig as well.

My father, the lifetime sum of whose big-game hunting had resulted, somewhat improbably, in his taking two mule deer, that alligator, and a *polar bear,* had decided one day, pretty much out of what one might generally term the "blue," that he wanted to hunt wild pigs. So on our first morning out he spotted for himself a reddish boar standing at the head of a draw and made a rather noteworthy dead-center shoulder shot of something over 150 downhill yards—the *end* of which, I might add, has yet to be heard. That left us with one genuine trophy boar—a pig with tusks over two inches long, measured from the gum line to the tip along the outside curve—to be taken by my friend Ellis Wilson, who had come all the way from Boise to join the hunt with us. Then a pig for me after Ellis had taken his.

And now that I come to think of it, I am not a 100 percent positive I can say what there actually *is* about the hunting of wild pigs, especially here in North America where they seem no more than strangers come to visit. The wild pig in assorted shapes does range throughout Europe and Asia and Africa, but in the entire Western Hemisphere the only native game that comes at all close to the pig is the peccary, a mammal really no more than "piglike" and in many ways closer to the ruminants than the swine.

The wild boar of Eurasia and North Africa, *Sus scrofa,* the progenitor of modern domestic swine, is the most ancient and primitive of even-toed ungulates. He is decidedly nonruminant, an eater of everything—as is man—who—again like man—learned successfully to tolerate some of the most widely disparate circumstances nature had to throw at him. Yet his home is not here; and the question lingers: What, exactly, am I doing hunting him in this New World?

Much, of course, does connect me—and most of us—to him.

Forty thousand years prior to our coming to North America, one of us daubed the wild boar's image onto his cave wall at Altamira in what is now Spain, then stepped back to contemplate his work. He represented the pig leaping in attack, its bristles raised, and hoped the painting would in some way deliver him unharmed from any encounter with the boar's nearly mystical tusks, or at least make the task of finding the pig when he set out to hunt it just a little easier.

The Assyrians, Egyptians, Greeks, and Romans also left behind for us their own images of the boar and the hunt for him, affixing him to temple walls, glazed amphoras, the sides of sarcophagi in bas-relief, *chalcedony scaraboids,* and the emblem the Roman Twentieth Legion wore when they marched into Britain.

Wild boar, or beings who assumed their shape (in, it would seem, much the same manner as the "bear-men" of the North American Indians assumed the shape of grizzlies), were forever—often quite literally *forever*—laying low the heroes, gods, demigods, and devils of ancient mythology. Vishnu became a boar to slay the demon Hiranyaksha and free the land from a flood. The dark twin Set, as a boar, kills his brother Osiris, the Egyptian god of the underworld. The Syrians' Tammuz, the Greeks' Adonis, Cretan

Zeus, Carmanor the son of Dionysius, Apollo's son Idmon the Argive, all had their lives taken by wild boars.

Great Ancaeus, the helmsman for the Argonauts, survived the many perils of the voyage for the Golden Fleece only on the very day of his return to be killed in his own vineyard as he tried to drive a boar from it. Another Ancaeus, of ever-bucolic Arcadia, was castrated and disemboweled during the famous hunt for the huge rampaging boar of Calydon, in which the virgin Atalanta—who had been suckled by a she-bear and raised in a clan of hunters, and who began the day of the hunt by shooting dead a pair of centaurs who meant to take liberties with her—drew first blood from the boar with her arrow and was awarded its hide and tusks after it lay dead. Outside Greece, it was for the love of Grainne, the daughter of King Cormac of Ireland, that the legendary Celtic hunter and warrior Finn Mac Coul made himself into a wild boar to kill his nephew Diarmait O Duibhne.

If there is a common root to all these tales of death by boars, it would seem to be that most grow out of the seasonal death of bright summer, or the reaping of the crop at summer's end, and the relentless onslaught of winter's dark. In these stories it is given to the wild boar to come, in the ancient lunar year's thirteenth and final month, bearing in his coat of bristles the solstice's fearful darkness.

Now darkness was almost upon us. Before the last of the shooting light on the hunt's second day, Ellis and August and I had spent most of an hour sitting far up on one side of a canyon, silently watching two enormous boars stir in the thick black sage on the other. The pigs would show us only the tops of their black backs, or their rumps moving behind a bush, so we never had a shot. Smaller pigs had come out into the open draw below us to begin the feeding that would carry them from evening through the night and to barely past dawn, but Ellis was set firmly on a trophy. When the big boars got into sage so thick we could no longer see any sign of them, we climbed out of the canyon and back up to the ridge to start our way in, leaving the boars for another time.

We were halfway down the ridge, with its oaks and pines,

when we saw the sounder of wild pigs out in the open field below us. They stood in the cold shadow the ridge cast in the sunset, nearly a dozen animals, all large adults. The largest stood alone at the rear of the sounder, stood tall and lean-looking, his thick mane of bristles caping his neck and shoulders. We worked our way quietly down the slope to where Ellis could get a rest for his rifle.

When Ellis's .30-caliber bullet tore a hole in his heart, the big boar, without a squeal or a grunt, swung away from the rest of the sounder as it made for cover, describing for himself a wide galloping arc through the field's tall green grass before collapsing. By the time we got down to him, the crescent moon had begun to rise. We could see that he was reddish black in color with most of the features of a pure wild boar and with 2½-inch curves of lower tusks that gleamed in the moonlight, but no brighter than Ellis's grin.

A boar's upper tusks are there only to safeguard and sharpen his lower set, those honed bottom tusks being the instruments he employs to deal with the world. Sir Robert Stephenson Smyth Baden-Powell (1857–1941), First Baron Baden-Powell, founder of the Boy Scout movement, and the then colonel responsible for the 215-day British defense of Mafeking against the Boers during the South African War of 1899–1902, who was as well an ardent practitioner of the mounted sport of pig-sticking while quartered as a young officer in India, wrote that the mark of a perfect pair of boar's tusks was that when placed base to base and tip to tip they would describe a perfect circle. It was this crescent shape of his tusks which made the boar sacred to the Moon for the Greeks.

In the matter of hunting the wild boar, the Athenian essayist Xenophon, in the fifth century B.C., recommended in his hunting treatise *Cynegeticus* that the Greek boar hunter use a spear with a fifteen-inch blade, "keen as a razor," with copper teeth projecting from the middle of the socket to stop the boar from running up the length of the shaft when struck and held by the hunter. He also advised the use of "Indian, Cretan, Locrian, and Laconian" hounds, "prepared to fight the beast," for hunting dogs. The boar was to be driven from its lair and caught in a purse net, but if it escaped before being killed and attacked a hunter who was without benefit of a spear, that hunter was to hurl himself to the ground and grasp the underbrush to prevent the boar from getting its tusks underneath him and leaving him looking like poor Ancaeus, *a* or *b*. It was the obligation of the other hunters, then, to drive the boar off their companion at the earliest opportunity.

The nobility of Europe continued to hunt the pig in much this same style for the next two thousand years, until the use of firearms became widespread. Certain ancient beliefs about the boar were carried over from Xenophon to the second-century A.D. *Omasticon* of Julius Pollux, even to *The Gentleman's Recreator* of 1686. It was believed, for instance, that "very fiery heat exists in the beast," so that just the touch of his tusks to the coat of a hound could send that animal up in flames, and that even a dead boar retained so much heat that if you placed a few dog hairs on a tusk of his, the hairs would shrivel up as if placed on a "hot iron." (And for all I know, this may be no fable. No one I know of has ever taken the time to lay a dog's hairs on the tusk of a dead boar to observe the result scientifically. As for there being a *fire* in the beast, this I do know to be assuredly true.)

In India the pastime of pig-sticking grew out of *bear*-sticking when the eighteenth century saw a dip in the subcontinent's bear population that was inimical to the continuance of proper sport. Pig-sticking, however, proved an excellent substitute. It was done on horseback with only "tough, springy, seasoned, male bamboo" spears with triangular steel heads, preferably the products of Thornhill, Rogers, or Wilkinson, all reputable manufacturers of English steel. A pig was *never* to be shot.

From Baden-Powell's most illustrative descriptions of the hunts they were apparently large-scale affairs conducted at five o'clock on spring mornings—following rousing nights in the cook tent that involved repeated "goes" of claret and choruses of boar-hunting songs gleaned from back numbers of the *Oriental Sporting Magazine*. A hundred "coolies" (who in unguarded moments might offhandedly be referred to as "niggers") would be assembled and sent off to beat the pig cover, and frequently be severely gored. Three or four mounted hunters would be stationed at the ready, weapons in hand, and when a boar was "reared" and its line of escape made clear, the word "Ride!" would be given and they would charge hell-bent after the pig for the honor of "first spear." Often these hunts would be attended by large parties of spectators seated in howdahs on the backs of elephants.

As the lead hunter drew up on the boar, the pig was apt to "jink" off, as Baden-Powell would have it, into some Indian dirt farmer's corn or millet crop, which of course necessitated the rider's trampling in after it with his horse. Sometimes the boar would go to ground in an area that was "unridable," and here the solution was to set the cover ablaze and burn the pig out. If in the process a coolie or two were "roasted alive," at least they had the satisfaction of knowing they died in the cause of the "king of sports." The slightest infraction of the strict rules of riding etiquette by any of the hunters could be most sternly penalized by the imposition of such fines as "one dozen of champagne," and no doubt the final spearing to death of the pig was greeted by the politest of applause from the gallery on elephant back.

The British deigned to consider the wild pig an opponent *worthy* of them because of its intelligence, hardiness, and ferocity. A wild boar would gore and even knock down a horse during a hunt. It showed little or no fear of dogs, camels, or even elephants and was not only said to be indifferent to the presence of tigers about it in the jungle, but actually had been observed to have *killed* them on occasion in fights. It was these splendid qualities as a game animal—and maybe something else that I was trying to understand about it—which brought the wild pig to North America and California.

In the state domestic swine had been drifting loose and going feral since Mission days. The pure wild blood in the California herds, though, can be traced to the Ural Mountains. The somewhat hazy line of its genealogy seems to begin there and runs to an Englishman, George Gordon Moore, who in 1912 had thirteen wild Russian pigs, via an agent in Berlin, shipped to Hoopers Bald in western North Carolina. There he is said to have kept the pigs penned in on 600 acres until in the early 1920s a bona fide pig-sticking match could be organized on the by then sixty to one hundred animals. During the commotion of the hunt, it is purported that many of the pigs quite rightly crashed through their split-rail enclosure and escaped into the surrounding hills, where they survive to this day. Enough remained after the hunt, however, for Moore in 1925 or '26 to arrange for three wild boars and nine wild sows to be transported to California from Hoopers Bald and turned loose on Monterey County's San Francisquito Ranch, now known as the San Carlos Ranch—and *not* on William Randolph Hearst's San Simeon Ranch, a common fallacy often given credence by any number of natterwits, myself, alas, formerly included.

Joining up with the feral hogs already in place, the wild pigs, being pigs, bred and then spread, deploying themselves into the grazing, rooting, scavenging, and acorn-collecting niche in California's ecology once occupied by the grizzly bear and the hunting-gathering North American Indian, both lately eradicated.

No foolproof method exists for determining a pure wild boar in California from one crossbred to a feral pig. A wild pig does have thirty-six chromosomes and a domestic one thirty-eight, and interbreeding them produces offspring with thirty-seven. Yet let the generation of offspring interbreed, and you can achieve piglets with thirty-six, thirty-seven, or thirty-eight chromosomes, whatever fancy strikes that molecule of pig DNA, *x*s and *y*s doled out in a mélange of genetic randomness. This is not to say, though, that a wild boar is without a definite *look* to him.

He will stand taller than the ordinary chuffy lard hog from which most feral pigs derive. There will be an angularity and slimness to his hips, and his head will be long and slender-snouted, with the eyes set far back to protect them while he roots—although his vision is so shamefully poor this seems hardly worth the trouble. His ears will be erect and heavily haired, and his long, bristly pelage will range in color from reddish brown to gray-black, with gray hairs increasing over his belly and jowls in a grizzled pattern known as *agouti* after the color scheme of a tropical American rodent.

A wild boar will possess a mane, or "comb," of long, erect bristles along his neck and spine, and in a cold California winter he may even grow back a thick underfur of curly wool like that carried by those of his breed still at large in the forests and mountains of Europe and Asia. Under his hide, which if you have it tanned for leather after killing him you will find thoroughly crosshatched with the scars of old battles, he carries an inch-thick plate of keratin, the stuff of hooves and horns. It extends on either side of his body, back from his shoulders to his last ribs, and shields his vital organs from the tusks of other boars when he fights them during the breeding time. If you slap your hand on a boar's side when you find him lying dead in a green field at dusk, as Ellis did, this keratin shield will boom for you like a hollow log being drummed. Care should be taken, though, in touching a hand to the tusks before they have cooled.

The next morning was the last of the hunt, and white fog filled the big river valley far below us. Up here in the hills it was clear and continuingly cold, and by the time August and I decided to try going down through a dense hillside of black sage where the pigs bedded during the day, I had already missed chances at two good boar. We were ready by then to try anything, and there were unquestionably pigs in this sage. We were assured of this because as August and I moved down through the chest-high brush we could smell them. We could smell them, we could hear them snuffling and grunting and snorting all around us, we could see them shaking the brush as they moved, we could do everything but get a clear shot at one. The pigs knew this. We tried throwing rocks to kick them out, we stood talking loudly to kick them out, we even tried kicking them, or at least the brush they were lying behind, to kick them out. They abided yet.

At one point up on the ridgeline a sow and two piglets had broken across the narrow trail in front of me, then a minute later had come three yearling hogs, the perfect eating size, no more than five yards from me, getting airborne as they leaped the gap in the brush. It was like trying to hunt pigs as quail, and I began to consider the option of a 12-gauge with double-aught loads. Stalking them in the brush, though—even with the knowledge that a pig may turn dangerous only when he is crippled and angry, and then he may start stalking *you*—I almost longed for the reassurance of a stout boar spear, a purse net, and a Laconian hound at my side.

In hunting wild pigs in California you try every legal and fair-chase means at hand because you never know what will work next, or at what precise moment a pig will decide to do . . . *God knows what*. When it looked, however, as if the pigs were going to do nothing, and nothing we could do was going to work, August and I started the long climb back up the ridge and in. The day seemed done, but I could still feel my heart fluttering happily from having been in that sage with wild pigs, and that said everything to me about what I *was* doing in this New World hunting them. Or nearly everything.

When August's people first came into the Diablo Range of California three generations past and only a little before the wild boar reached Hoopers Bald, it was in a spring wagon, the worldly goods they brought with them including one shotgun and $400 in gold in a sack to buy a ranch from a homesteader. When my people came to California three generations past, it was on a clipper that had rounded the Horn one jump ahead of a potato blight. And this is where I abide yet.

Still, there are times when it is my secret suspicion that North America is not where I belong. There are subtleties to this land and its game, rules and rites for the hunting of it which were refined to a very high degree over the course of tens of thousands of years by people far different from mine, and which at times I am sure I shall never be able to fathom. My links to North America's game seem on occasion tenuous and outside me, as if I were slated forever to be no more than a dabbler on this continent—or worse, a barger like some subaltern "quartered" in a foreign locale, who, ignorant of all local custom and long-standing tradition, sets out to remake a land by stamping his image onto it with a sixteen-pound maul. Maybe *this*, at last, is what there is about hunting wild pigs in California—and maybe this is the something else the men who brought them here felt also—the way it ties me to what I sometimes see as my true past, my only tribal memory, which is from a place other than this.

And that is enough forced *mal du pays* for one day. Obviously, this North America is where I now am, am a part of, and mean to stay. There really is no longer any "there" left to return to, even if I actually wanted to. It's been gone since before the Greeks, maybe even before the Egyptians. I would probably have to go back to somewhere around the time the paint was still tacky in that cave to reclaim it. This is where the boar is now, too, and he has learned to fit it well. Perhaps I should no longer think of him as a stranger here; and perhaps, learning gracefully from him, neither should I think of myself as one. It may very well be that any place we hunt, if we do it honorably, becomes our real home. I can remember many far places in this world that became "mine" after I hunted them. It could be, if we will understand one thing, that we are strangers nowhere in this world. In our long past as hunters we were nomads, and it must be that we remain nomads today. We can ultimately possess no animal or piece of ground. We can only be possessed by it.

That does seem a portentous load to try to make a poor wild pig lug around with him—though certainly no more burdensome than a solstice—yet as I said, there is just *something* about hunting him. If you let him, he can root right into your thoughts the way he roots into the soil of a hillside, turning it all over to expose it to the sun. Or you can, as August and I did as we climbed up the ridge, see a singular boar looking as big and black as an Angus bull break from the cover you were just rocking, cross the canyon, and be over the next ridge in an instant, and forget all else as you give chase.

By the time you top that next ridge the boar will be three hundred yards away, running across an open field. The first shot from your .375 will kick up the dirt at his heels. Your next will be too far ahead of him. You'll try a third and a fourth heavy bullet; but when they also miss him clean, the wild boar will make it to the cover of a ravine, gone to ground.

And in that moment of his disappearance he will become what he can never cease being. He will be history.

Buff!

They saw the buffalo after killing the elephant. The professional hunter switched off the engine and eased out of the battered olive Land-Rover, carrying his binoculars. His client slipped out on the other side, and one of the trackers in the back, without needing to be told, handed his .300 down to him. The client fed the 200-grain Noslers into the magazine and put the 220-grain solid into the chamber, locking the bolt as the professional hunter glassed the buffs.

It was nearly sunset, and already in the back of the Land-Rover lay the heavy curves of ivory, darkened and checked by decades of life, the roots bloodied. They had found the old bull elephant under a bright acacia late in the afternoon, having tracked him all day on foot. He was being guarded by two younger bulls, his askaris; *and when the client made the brain shot, red dust puffing off the side of the elephant's head, and the old bull dropped, the young ones got between and tried to push him back onto his feet, blocking the insurance rounds. But the bullet had just missed the bull's brain, lodging instead in the honeycomb of bone in the top of his skull, and he came to and regained his feet, and they had to chase him almost a mile, firing on the run, until he went down for good. By then it was too late to butcher out the dark red flesh, so they left that task until the next morning when they would return with a band of local villagers and carry out everything edible, down to the marrow in the gigantic bones. They took only the tusks that afternoon. Still, when they finally reached the Land-Rover again they were very tired, pleased with themselves, and ready only for a long drink back in camp.*

So when on the way to that drink the professional hunter spotted a bachelor herd of Cape buffalo (with two exceptionally fine bulls in it), it was all a bit much, actually. Yet he motioned his client to come around behind the Land-Rover to his side anyway, and, crouching, they worked behind some low cover toward the bulls, the Mbogos.

The first rule they give you about dangerous game is to get as close as you possibly can before firing—then get a hundred yards closer. *When the professional felt they had complied with this stricture, to the extent that they could clearly see yellow-billed oxpeckers hanging beneath the bulls' flicking ears, feeding on ticks, he got his client into a kneeling position and told him to take that one bull turned sideways to them: put the solid into his shoulder, then pour on the Noslers. It was then that the client noticed that the professional was backing him up on this bull buffalo with a pair of 8 X German binoculars instead of his customary .470 Nitro Express double rifle. The professional just shrugged and said, "You should be able to handle this all right by yourself."*

Taking a breath, the client hit the buffalo in the shoulder with the solid and staggered him. The bull turned to face them and the client put two quick Noslers into the heaving chest, aiming right below the chin, and the buffalo collapsed. As the client reloaded, the second fine bull remained where he was, confused and belligerent, and the professional hunter urged his client to take him too: "Oh my yes, him too." *This bull turned also after the first solid slammed into his shoulder, and lifted his head toward them, his scenting nose held high. Looking into a wounded Cape buffalo's discomfortingly intelligent eyes is something like looking down the barrel of a loaded .45 in the hands of a mean drunk. That is a time when you have to be particularly mindful of what you are doing out there in Africa and make your shots count—especially when your professional hunter, already suspect because of the way he talks English and the fact he wears short pants, who is backing you up now on dangerous game with a pair of 8 X German binoculars, especially when he leans over and whispers calmly, "Look: he's going to come for us."*

Another careful breath and the client placed two more bullets neatly into the bull's chest beneath his raised chin, just the way he had on the first one, except this bull did not go down. That left the client with one round in his rifle, and as he was about to squeeze it off he wondered if there would be any time left afterward for him either to reload or to make a run for it. For now, however, there was this enraged buffalo that had to be gotten onto the ground somehow, and all the client could really be concerned about was holding his rifle steady until the sear broke and the cartridge fired and the bullet sped toward the bull—but just before the rifle fired its last round the buffalo lurched forward and fell with a bellow, stretching his black muzzle out in the dirt. Then he was silent.

Standing up slowly, the client and the professional hunter moved cautiously toward the two downed buffalo (the rest of the small herd now fled), to find them both dead. Only then in the dwindling light did they see that one of the first bull's horns, the horn that had been turned away from them when the client first shot, had been broken away in recent combat and a splintered stump was all that remained. He had been a magnificent bull at one time, but at least the second bull's horns were perfect, beautifully matched sweeps of polished black horn, almost fifty inches across the spread. And there, both men stooping to squint at it, glittered a burnished half-inch steel ball bearing buried in the horn boss covering the bull's head like a helmet. The ball bearing had once served as a musketball fired out of an ancient muzzle-loader. Whoever the native hunter was who fired it, he must have had one overpowering lust for buffalo meat, and for buffalo hunting. What became of him after he shot and missed with his quixotic weapon at a ludicrously close range is probably something best not speculated upon.

When I first heard that story I was a boy of nine or ten. It was told by a gentleman of my acquaintance (a man who taught me how to hunt then, and with whom I have had the pleasure of hunting ever since), who had experienced it on a safari to Tanzania twenty years ago. Like most hunting tales, it has been twice and three times told since, yet unlike some others it has never grown tedious with the tellings, only aging gracefully. Every time I hear the gentleman's excitement in telling it, and see the massive head on the wall with the steel ball shining in the horn, it explains something to me of why a person could get daffy about hunting Cape buffalo. Its power as a legend was such that it sent me off to East Africa once to hunt buffalo myself.

Black, sparsely haired, nearly a ton in weight, some five feet high at the shoulder, smart and mean as a whip, and with a set of immense but elegant ebony horns that sweep down, then up and a little back, like something drawn with a French curve, to points sharp enough to kill a black-maned lion with one blow—horns that can measure almost five feet across the outside spread—the African Cape buffalo is, along with the Indian water buffalo and the Spanish fighting bull, one of the three great wild cattle of the world. Of these three, though, the water buffalo has been largely domesticated—with a few animals transplanted to Australia and South America having reverted to the untamed state—and the fighting bull's wildness is the product of over two thousand years of men having restricted his breeding to keep the blood of the aurochs still running through his veins. The Cape buffalo alone among these has never had any dealings with men, other than of the most terminal kind.

With his ferocious temper, treacherous intellect, and stern indifference to the shocking power of all but the most outlandishly large-caliber rifles, the Cape buffalo is routinely touted as the most dangerous member of the African Big Five (which also includes the lion, leopard, black rhino, and elephant). Whether he is or not all depends, as does almost everything under the sun, on what you mean. He is certainly not as sure to charge as a rhino, or as swift as the carnivorous cats; and in the words of a sporting journalist I know, "nobody every got *wounded* by an elephant." But the buff is swift enough; and when he makes up his mind to charge, especially when injured, there is no animal more obdurately bent on finishing a fight. In open flat country he may present no serious threat to a hunter properly armed, but you seldom encounter him on baseball-diamond-like surroundings—rather more often he'll be in some swampy thicket or dense forest where he is clever enough to go to cover, and fierce enough to come out of it.

The best measure of the Cape buffalo's rank as a big-game animal may simply be the kind of esteem professional hunters hold him in. It is a curious fact of the sporting life that big, tall, strapping red-faced chaps who make their livings trailing dangerous game all come in time to be downright maudlin about which animals they feel right about hunting. Most, therefore, first lose their taste for hunting the big cats, so that while they will usually do their best to get a client his one and only lion, their hearts will not entirely be in it: the predatory cats in their appetites for meat and sleep and sex are simply too close to us for comfort. Then there is the rhino, the hulking, agile, dumb, blind, sad, funny, savage, magnificent Pleistocene rhino who every day is getting hammered just that much closer to the Big Jump we term *extinction:* under present conditions only a raving criminal sociopath could feel good about destroying one more specimen of that fleeting arrangement of molecules we term *rhino.*

Of the Big Five, then, that leaves only the elephant and the Cape buffalo to feel at all right about hunting, and to my knowledge hardly any real professional hunter, unless he has lost interest in hunting altogether, ever totally loses his taste for giving chase to these two. There is no easy way to hunt elephant and Cape buffalo—you must be able to walk for miles on end, know how to follow animal signs well, and be prepared to kill an animal who can just as readily kill you—and this makes them the two greatest challenges for taking good trophy animals, and the two most satisfying: something about hunting them will get into a hunter's blood and stay. To offer one further bit of testimony on behalf of the buff, consider the widely known piece of jungle lore that the favorite sport of *elephants* is chasing herds of Cape buffalo round and round the bush, and the buff's position as one of the world's great big-game animals seems secure.

Which is why I wanted to hunt buff, and went to do so in the southwestern corner of Kenya near Lake Victoria, in the Chepa-lungu Forest on top of the Soit Ololol Escarpment and above the

Great Rift Valley, to arguably the loveliest green spot in all green Masailand, and one which I dearly hated—to begin with, anyway.

To find buffalo there we would put on cheap canvas tennis shoes (because they were the only things that would dry overnight) and slog every day into the dim wet forest (filled with butterflies and spitting cobras, birds and barking bushbucks, gray waterbucks and giant forest hogs, rhino, elephant, and buffalo), penetrating a wall of limbs and vines and deep green leaves woven as tight as a Panama hat, through which one could see no more than ten feet in any direction. On going in, the advice given me by my professional hunter, John Fletcher (who is today, I hear, a grower of onions on the slopes of Mount Kenya), was that in the event of my stumbling onto a sleeping buffalo (as well I might) I should try to shoot the animal dead on the spot and ask questions later. It took only a momentary lack of resolve at such a juncture, he assured me, to give a buffalo ample opportunity to spring up and winnow you right down. And that was the root cause of my hating this beautiful African land: it scared the hell out of me, and I hated being scared.

As we hunted the buffalo, though, a change did begin to come over me. We had had unheard-of luck on cats at the outset of the safari, so that at dawn on my fifth morning of hunting in Africa, while concealed in a blind, I had taken a very fine leopard as he came to feed on a hanging bait; and then, the evening of the same day, we had incredibly gotten up on an extremely large lion, *simba mkubwa sana* in the eager words of the trackers, and I had broken his back with my .375, establishing what may very well have been some sort of one-day East African record for cats, which we duly celebrated that night. So when our hangovers subsided two days later, we moved off from that more southern country near Kilimanjaro to the Block 60 hunting area above the escarpment, assuming we would take quickly from the forest there a good buffalo (a bull with a spread over forty inches wide—ideally forty-five or better, with fifty inches a life's ambition—along with a full, tightly fitted boss), then move on again to the greater-kudu country we had, until the luck with cats, not hoped to have time to reach.

Instead of a good buffalo in short order, though, we had to go into that forest every day for two weeks, first glassing the open country futilely at daybreak, then following into the cover the tracks the buffalo left when they had moved back in before dawn, their night's grazing done. In that forest where the light sifted down as if into deep water, we picked our way for two weeks over rotting timber and through mud wallows, unseen animals leaping away from us on all sides, creeping our way forward until we could hear low grunts, then the sudden flutter of oxpeckers (more euphoniously known as tickbirds) flaring up from the backs of the buffalo they were preening, and then the flutter of alarmed Cape buffalo flaring up as well, snorting, crashing so wildly away (yet also unseen) through the dark forest that the soggy ground quivered and the trees were tossed about as if in a windstorm and the report of wood being splintered by horns could be heard for hundreds of yards through the timber. That was the sound a breeding herd of cows, calves, and young bulls made as they fled; but other times there would be the flutter of oxpeckers and no crashing afterward, only a silence the booming of my heart seemed to fill, and we knew we were onto a herd of bulls, wise old animals who were at that moment slipping carefully away from us, moving off with inbred stealth, or maybe stealthily circling back to trample us into the dirt! For much of those two weeks, then, I saw things in that forest through a glaze of fear as ornate as the rose window in a medieval French cathedral.

I discovered, however, that you can tolerate fear roaring like a train through your head and clamping like a limpet to your heart for just so long; and sometime during those two weeks I ceased to be *utterly* terrified by the black forms in the bush, and instead grew to be excited by them, by the chance of encountering them, by the possibility that my life was actually on the line in there: my heart still boomed, but for a far different reason now. What was going on in that forest, I saw, was a highly charged game of skill: if you played it wrong, you might be killed; but if you played it just right, you got to do it over again. No more than that. But when something like that gets into your blood, the rest of life comes to lack something you never knew before it was supposed to have.

I believe it got into mine one evening when we chased a breeding herd in and out of the forest for hours, jumping it and driving it ahead of us, trying to get a good look at one of the bulls in it. Finally we circled ahead of the buffalo into a clearing of chest-high grass where they had to cross in front of us. We hunkered down and watched them as they came out. The bull appeared at last, but he was only a young seed bull, big-bodied but not good in the horns yet. As we watched him pass by, a tremendous cow buffalo, the herd matriarch, walked out, maybe sixty yards from us, and halted. Then she turned and stared directly our way.

If she feels her calf or her herd is threatened, the cow buffalo is probably as deadly an animal as there is; and at that moment I found myself thinking that that was just the most wonderful piece of knowledge in the world to have. It meant she might charge, and, may God forgive me, I *wanted* her to. Very much.

"All right," John Fletcher whispered, carrying his William G. Evans .500 Nitro Express—with two 578-grain bullets in it and two more cartridges, like a pair of Montecristo cigars, held in his left palm under the forearm—carrying it across his body like a laborer's shovel, "All right," he whispered, "we'll stand now, and she'll run off. Or she'll charge us." No more than that.

So we stood, John Fletcher, I, and the trackers behind us, and the buffalo cow did not budge. We could see her thinking, weighing the odds, her nostrils twitching. John Fletcher and I brought our rifles up at the same instant without a word and took aim: as soon as she started forward, I knew I was going to put a .375 into the center of her chest, exactly where my cross hairs were, and if she kept coming I would put in another, and another after that if I could, but I would not run. As the seconds passed, I felt more and more that, for perhaps one of the few times in my life, I was behaving correctly, no fear clouding my vision. To know absolutely that you are capable of standing your ground is a sparkling sensation.

Then the cow snorted and spun away from us, following the herd, her calculations having come up on the negative side for her. I took my finger off the trigger then, and carefully reset the safety. And all the trackers came up and one by one clapped me on the back, smiling their nervous African smiles, as if to say, "You did well." I was glad we hadn't had to kill the cow after all.

Yet, when at first light on our fourteenth day of buffalo

hunting we reached the edge of a small dewy field and spotted three good bulls feeding in it a hundred yards away and I got my first chance to kill a Cape buffalo, I did not kill him at all well. Though he was the smallest-bodied buffalo of the three, old and almost hairless, his horns swept out nearly forty-five inches, much farther than the other two's, and when I fired—low, near his heart, but not near enough—he began to trot in a slow circle as the two younger bulls came past us at an oblique angle, just visible in the edge of my scope. I shot him again and again, anywhere, and again, and Fletcher fired once, and at last he went down and I had to finish him on the ground. There was still, I had to admit, after the bull lay dead and all my ammunition was gone, enough fear left in me to prevent my behaving completely correctly.

We went on hunting Cape buffalo after that right up to my last day on safari—John Fletcher looking for an even better trophy for me, and me looking to make up for the first kill, hoping there was still time. On the last morning of hunting we flushed a bushbuck, and I had only the briefest second to make one of the toughest running shots I have ever tried and took the sturdy little antelope through the heart as he stretched into full flight. Suddenly I was very anxious to try another buffalo before leaving Africa.

We found the herd that evening when John and I and my photographer friend William Cullen were out alone, the trackers back helping break camp. The buffalo had been drifting in and out of the forest all that gray highland afternoon with us behind them, following their tracks—a bull's cloven print, as big as a relish tray, standing out from all the others. It seemed that we had lost the herd for good, though, until a small boy, no older than four or five, wearing a rough cotton toga and carrying a smooth stick, appeared startlingly out of the bush before us and asked in Masai if we would like to kill a buffalo.

The little child led us along a forest trail to the edge of the trees, where he pointed across an open glade to the bull. The Cape buffalo bull, his tight boss doming high above his head, stood in the herd of ten or fifteen other animals in the nearing dark, only a few yards from heavy cover—in which in no more than half a dozen running steps he could be completely concealed. John Fletcher, for one, was something more than slightly aware of this. He remembered too well how I had killed my first bull, and though he'd said nothing, he knew how much the buffalo had spooked me. If I wounded this bull now and he made it into the forest with the light going, and the second rule they give you for dangerous game being that you follow all wounded animals in . . . well . . . Fletcher looked at me carefully. There was no denying it was a good bull, though, and the trackers and camp staff would want some more meat to take home, and there was still a little light, and *and oh bloody hell!*

As we knelt at the edge of the forest, Fletcher whispered to me, "Relax, now. Keep cool. Take your time. Are you ready? Are you all right?"

I glanced at him, then back at the buffalo. I was, at that moment, as all right as I was ever going to get. This was where it counted; this was what it was all about; this was exactly what I'd come here for. It was in my blood now, only Fletcher might not know that. So I told him.

"Where," I whispered, easing the .375's safety off, "do you want me to shoot him, John?"

John Fletcher stared at me even harder then, but this time he whispered only, "There, in the shoulder."

You can see where a Cape buffalo's shoulder socket bulges under his hide, and if you travel through his body from there you will reach his spine where it dips down from his humped back to become his neck. That was where I laid my cross hairs, and when the 270-grain Nosler hit him there it broke his shoulder, then shattered his spine. And the bull was down, his muzzle stretched out along the short grass and the buffalo's bellowing death song (what the professionals call "music" when they hear it coming from a wounded bull laid up in cover) coming from his throat. The rest of the herd wheeled on us then, their eyes clear and wide and most uncattlelike, the smell of the bull's blood in their nostrils. I finished the bull with one more round to the neck, and the herd was gone, vanishing as quickly as that bull could have vanished had my nerve not held and I had not behaved correctly.

That last night in camp, while the African staff jerked long strips of buffalo meat over the campfire to carry back to their wives and children, John Fletcher, William Cullen, and I sat in the dining tent and ate hot oxtail soup and slices of steaming boiled buffalo tongue and drank too much champagne and brandy, and laughed too much, too. We finished breaking camp at dawn the next morning and returned to Nairobi.

It seems I may have gone on with this story at too great a length already, but I wish I could go on even further to tell you all the other Cape buffalo stories I know, like the time John Fletcher was guiding a famous Mexican torero who meant to kill a bull buffalo with his curved steel sword—brought with him from Mexico for just that purpose—and what made him change his mind. Or how when you awoke in the middle of the night, needing relief, and stepped outside your canvas tent, you might make out, just there on that little rise at the edge of camp, the silhouettes of feeding buffalo against the cold stars as your urine steamed into the grass. Or how one of the many herds we chased out of the forest and across the green country led us into a spectacular cloudburst, and the storm wind began to swirl around so that our scent was swept in front of the fifty or sixty funeral-black animals and turned them back *on* us, and as they started forward I asked John what we did now, and he said lightly, "Actually, we might try shooting down the lead buffalo and climbing onto its back."

And I wish I could tell you the other stories without buffalo, how I saw a she-leopard in a tall tree battle a fish eagle over a dead impala. Or how when you killed an animal the sky would be a clean blue china bowl tipped over you and empty of birds out to the farthest horizon, but how in one minute a dozen naked-headed vultures would be circling lazily overhead, sprung from nowhere to create bare white bones in the tall grass. Or how we could be crossing country in the hunting car at forty miles an hour and one of the trackers in the back would drum on the cab roof, and when we stopped he would leap down and unerringly weave his way two hundred yards out into the scrub, and when we would catch up to him he would be pointing placidly at a bush where only then did we see the still-wet newborn gazelle curled underneath it in its nest, staring unblinking at us, the tracker seeming to have sensed its burgeoning life waiting out there.

But what I wish most of all is that I were back in those African highlands I grew to love dearly, hunting the Cape buffalo I grew to love too—probably still scared, but only enough to make me sense my true heart nested inside my chest and beating, telling me, over and over, of what I am capable.

Morning at Buffalo Ford

Then there is the other buffalo, as we know our native bison to be. When the buffalo had 3 million square miles of unfenced land to range over, Ernest Thompson Seton estimated that his number had been 25 to the square mile. Fences, however, seem an inevitability. The very first buffalo a European saw stood within a timber cage in the menagerie of Moctezuma in Tenochtitlán. There was a lesson about the wild to have been learned from that, even then.

In 75 million there were perhaps 75 white buffalo, a one-in-a-million shot. This made the white buffalo an object of veneration for the Indian, a creature sacred to the Sun God or simply "good medicine." Either way, killing one was a deed of profound significance. The carcass was given to a woman of the tribe, painted ceremonially by the medicine man to afford protection to her and those around her, to skin and dress the hide. Sometimes the chief would take the tanned robe and, armed with it, would ride into battle knowing invincibility.

Large-caliber bullets from the muzzles of army carbines put a stop to that, just as 420-grain bullets from the muzzles of Sharps rifles, with the help of plowshares and railroad lines, put a stop to the buffalo's free roaming. Lieutenant General Philip Henry Sheridan, commander of the Military Division of the Missouri and architect of the winter campaign against the Plains Indians, urged the striking of a medal in honor of the exterminators of the buffalo, one side to show a dead bison and the other an Indian broken in spirit by the loss of his rations; and from the Staked Plains to the Badlands the buffalo vanished, not little by little but by the thousands, then millions. It was as if a dam had been dynamited and, where only a short time before there had been a deep reservoir, there was now no more than the cracked mud of a dry bed. For a full decade after the buffalo were gone, a living was to be made on the prairies by the bone pilgrim who wandered it gathering up the whitened skeletons to sell for fertilizer, glue, and buttons.

The buffalo have come to be residents of parks now. Parks exist for a reason. They are where you put the wild, the Out There, when you're not really sure any longer where it actually belongs. Parks are a pretense. They are a pretense that nothing ever kills, nothing ever dies, nothing even threatens—at least not within sight of the visitors. Parks are where you are permitted to catch a trout on a barbless fly and return it to a river that is never to run with even a single drop of blood, because matters in this neck of the woods have been crowded into such a critical pass that blood cannot afford to be shed. A park is as fragile as an antique watch set under a bell jar, a watch that at any moment could stop ticking.

Saying all that, I should note that the first trout I ever caught on a fly was in a park. I had gone to school in West Yellowstone to learn how to present a fly to a trout and had then ventured uneasily into the park to try out my newfound knowledge.

Buffalo Ford on the Yellowstone River had been named with

some precision. As I headed down to the water on a September morning, flopping noisily in my new chest waders as my new fishing vest rattled and jangled, there was the smell of sulfur in the air, the bugling of an elk somewhere in the timber, and a gigantic buffalo bull standing shaggily in the middle of the trail. I made sure the berth I gave him was wide.

On the bank of the river I stretched the memory out of my leader, tied on and dressed my fly, and waded in over the stony bottom with—being new to fishing with a fly—what I saw as my fragile, bloodless tackle and bizarre garb. The icy water came nearly to the stainless-steel hemostats I had clipped to the bottom of my vest, and as my waders wrapped tight and cold around my legs I had the sensation that it was my turn to become an aqueous solution. Then I came to a riffle and in bad light got on my first native cutthroat.

He was a drifting brown smudge in the swift water, and suddenly my unease was gone and I wanted this trout to be mine. I maneuvered into position over the slick stones and cast the Royal Wulff over him. There was no hatch—the big ones of mayflies and caddis and salmon flies all come and gone—and the trout were nymphing on the bottom. Yet I wanted this first trout to be on a dry fly and was determined to take him no other way.

After about an hour of serving up the imitation to that cutthroat and every other cutthroat in sight, with no takers, I cast the fly over his riffle for an untold time and dully watched it drift into invisibility in the lambent glare coming off the moving water. Then I lifted the rod tip as I had done so many times already, and this time, do not ask me why, the cutthroat leaped into the air.

The combat, witnessed by two ravens the size of mopeds, standing attentively on a nearby gravel bar, lasted four superb minutes while the trout turned every way but loose. He fought marvelously, and when I brought him finally to hand he turned out to be fourteen inches of foul-hooked fish snagged behind the gill. Not even that, though, could take away from this moment for me, and promising myself to do better on the next one, I carefully unhooked him and sent him on his way unmolested so I could stalk another, stumbling as I went over a wide wedge of cutthroat earnestly feeding on the nymphs and larvae my wading had stirred up.

I landed four cutthroat trout that day, fought another for ten minutes to a "long-line release," and, moving downstream, struck and took the fly away from at least six more before pausing long enough to check the hook and see that the point had been broken off it somewhere upriver without my knowing. At its end, though, it was as fine a day in the Out There as I could recall, and I would exchange it for no other. (Angling for trout seems to do that to your prose.)

That's what I was thinking as I left the river, that it had not been a bad day for one spent in a park, and that maybe parks were not quite the aberrations I tried to make them out to be, were not such distortions of the wild and the natural order of things after all. Then I made it back up to the road where all the cars were parked, and across the black asphalt on a soft yellow hillside I saw something that sent all these warm new feelings up in a sorry puff of dirty smoke.

The bull buffalo I had seen fit to detour around in the morning was lying now in the hillside's grass. And encircling him at no more than two yards' remove was a band of not fewer than forty park visitors, armed with Instamatics as the badge of their tribe. There were turret-lathe operators, federal employees, mothers with babes in arm, Little Leaguers, Social Security recipients, color-field painters, cocktail waitresses, professors of Baroque architecture, and Saints of the Latter-Day, all closing in for close-ups. These were not necessarily bad people, just very silly and ignorant ones. They had only gathered around the buffalo because he had been so near the highway.

I stood watching, waiting for the buffalo to do something. The visitors were not about to leave until he did, and I am not sure what it was I wanted to see him do to them. Kill somebody? This had happened before in the park when a crowd had gathered around a buffalo and the buffalo had sullenly refused to perform for them—until somebody walked up to his backside and planted a swift kick there, instant death ensuing.

Maybe not that, but I could not bear the thought of his at last being driven off by the press of the visitors—scuttling for the safety of the timber. I could imagine forty identical postcards going out at sunset from forty different motels: "The buffalo in the park are meek as lambs; great photo opportunity," and the idea appalled me. Here was an animal who once in going wherever it had suited him had left trails across the Plains thirty feet wide in places and up to four feet deep. He had once owned a continent; but even holed up now in this park he was still being crowded by all the people. That he was letting them get away with it was for me the worst thing, though.

Nothing dies, nothing even threatens, I thought, silver-filled molars grinding against one another. Then some rock 'n' roll fanatic, shirtless in orange shorts and braved up with a beaded headband, squatted eighteen inches from the bull's muzzle to snap his photo. The bull stared at him, chewing a wad of prairie grass, and a dim buffalo thought began to smolder in his brain: This has gone far enough. He chewed a few seconds more, then sprang liquidly to his hooves without preamble. He raised his tail and lowered his mammoth head meaningfully, but the visitor didn't get it yet and just went on blithely exposing film. The buffalo charged like a steam locomotive jumping a track.

The orange-togged visitor reacted instinctively—at last—and threw himself backward as the buffalo's shaggy face thundered over him in a blur. Then he was on his feet and passing everything in sight as there was a general stampede down the hill to the tinted-glass security of the Detroit products. The buffalo halted two steps beyond where he had routed them all and turned to survey the headlong flight. Then he swished his tail and ambled off into the trees. He had just thrown one back.

So there it is, even in a park. The wild dies hard, hard as a yellow jacket trapped inside that bell jar with the watch, to *ping* and *ping* against the curved wall of the glass until you think it will shatter its way out. As you reach with a nervous hand to lift the jar and set it free, be careful—its sting remains sharp.

Trying to keep items of value stored hermetically away can be a daunting undertaking. The shine can still tarnish, and bright colors fade. A yellow jacket in amber, while no longer presenting a risk to people who know no better than to try to mishandle it, does not any longer fly. Nature's change and movement, of a kind far different from the unnatural frenetic sort so loved by this century, is the only constant. The Out There cannot be fixed to one place on a map and be expected to survive; it must first be a condition of our souls and understanding.

The Mandan were said to have offered many horses in exchange for the robe of a white buffalo. The benefits of its medicine they would then enjoy for a few years; but knowing it was not theirs to own, at the end of that time they would present the robe to the Great Spirit, to let him take it back with his rain and wind. When the robe had turned to dust, the memory of it remained around their and their children's hearts, blanketing them in warm whiteness.

The Cuban Flu

My reasons for going there remain cloudy to me, even after all this time. Certainly it was not so I could be of any assistance with the cane harvest or to be better able to understand the Revolution or any of the other more seemingly usual explanations for why someone heads south to there. It may have been no more than that for a few years from the late '70s to mid-1982 anyone *could,* without restriction, go there. So I went, to hunt wild fowl and fish and let some time pass.

Whenever I would first announce I was bound there for the purposes I have stated, I would invariably be greeted with choruses of "*Cuba?*"

"You mean," they would want to know, "the big island south

of Key West? You mean *Communist* Cuba? You mean, that is to say, *Fidel?*" I suppose that is what I did indeed mean. Most of these people knew little or nothing of Cuba, but I cannot say that after coming back from it I knew any more than they.

The trouble I still have with Cuba stems from the fact that I was there only twice—once in November of 1981 and again in February of 1982—each time for only a week, and each time only to the area around the Laguna de la Leche, a large saltwater lagoon more the color of Dijon mustard than of milk, lying on the north coast of the long narrow island near the town of Morón, itself some 250 miles east of Havana; and needless to say, the genuine *wealth* of information I gained this way never could clarify completely for me what it was I meant by "Cuba."

I certainly returned from Cuba with no insights into its form of government, its role in geopolitics, or its future as a state. What little I can say I did come to know about it concerned mostly the duck and dove hunting I found there, the small amount of large-mouth bass fishing I got in on Lake Redonda in the vicinity of the Laguna, and the few Cubans I met. I did come to know *that* about it, and that when I was in Cuba the week would always seem about two days too long. Yet after being home again for a month or two, I would find myself picking up the white and green registration card boldly identifying me as once having been a "distinguished guest" of the "Hotel MORON," and missing Cuba.

When I went to Cuba, one could still quite handily fly out of Florida and be on the island within three hours. The times I went, I would depart Fort Lauderdale early on a Sunday morning on board a well-loaded, well-maintained DC-3—a sort of tableau vivant from the pages of American aviation history—which after gaining altitude would swing out over the Gulf Stream and turn south. There would be islands below en route, Bimini and Andros, and the very turquoise, very shallow-looking Great Bahama Bank. The first sight I would have of Cuba would be the outer mangrove cays where the Old Bahama Channel ran, then the north shore. We would come in over the "Lagoon of Milk" and Redonda and Morón, then turn east to fly on another hundred miles to the airport at Camagüey.

Much of Cuba, I learned, was mountainous and hilly, but the adjoining central provinces of Camagüey and Ciego de Ávila (the "forest clearing of Ávila"), where Morón lay, were flat agricultural and ranch country. The roads ran out across this country in straight lines, and from the air you could see an occasional truck, but more often bicycles, moving along the packed red dirt or asphalt. As you came in above Camagüey, you would pass over many postrevolutionary housing constructions, some looking rather run-down, others (even *more* postrevolutionary perhaps) looking shiny and new; all, however, built in that same grand roofless plain proletarian ghastly deadening tradition of Bauhaus. Most of the housing you saw in the provinces, though, looked distinctly *"antes la revolución,"* expressing a predilection for shotgun houses with adobe-tile or thatched-palm roofs, *postigo* doors and *portales* to shade you from the sun, clean-swept floors, lighted TV sets, and sometimes a wall patched with rusting Coca-Cola signs.

Photography was frowned upon in the airport at Camagüey— other American sportsmen reporting having sighted the odd MiG or two parked on the field outside the small, somewhat aged, low pink terminal building on prior visits. There were no problems, however, with the gawking, jabbering, touristical use of cameras once away from it.

Clearing customs in Cuba was much like the process anywhere else in the world: public humiliation in the name of secure borders. (Why, the question would go in that uniquely abstruse accent of Spanish the Cubans possess, do you have in your suitcase *eleven* billed caps with adjustable plastic tabs on the backs and the name of an Indiana coal company printed on the crowns? Well, this one, the answer would come in Midwestern American spoken with the volume turned up so as to be more easily understood, is for duck hunting; this one for dove; this one for bass fishing; this one for luncheon. . . .) Yet to bring in a shotgun, all that was required was to give the tour agent out in Kingwood, Texas, the gun's serial number a week or two ahead of time; no restrictions were made on the number of shotgun shells you could import; and I can recall no one waving an AK-47 at me and demanding to see my papers and wanting to know what I was doing bringing a weapon *and* ammunition into Cuba as I would carry my shotgun and shells away from customs, past the framed photograph of Brezhnev, and outside to the big air-conditioned Spanish-made tourist bus parked on the tarmacadam under the hot sun.

The long afternoon ride from Camagüey to Morón, via the city of Ciego de Ávila, took me past many of the things that came to seem "Cuban" to me. There were the green pastures with solitary ceiba trees bulking leaflessly against the horizon; clusters of tall royal palms, their bark the color of newly poured concrete, standing up to spanking breezes coming in off the Atlantic; goats methodically cropping the long grass along the road's shoulder; barefoot boys riding lean horses; old whitewashed haciendas set back in cool groves; vultures sailing noiselessly overhead; a black woman smoking a pipe, shooing the chickens back into her dusty yard; dewlapped Brahman cattle grazing behind a three-wire fence; a bleached pig skull lying on a rusting tin roof; towering smoke stacks billowing huge clouds of sulfurous black smoke into the tropic sky; fields of cane and rows of citrus trees; and every so often a political slogan strung out along the highway on a series of billboards like a Marxist-Leninist model of the Burma Shave sign.

In Cuba I would hunt out of the Hotel Morón, which resembled every large men's dormitory built on the campus of every major United States university in the mid sixties. It was an unquestionably weird sensation to know I was in *Cuba,* with all that it had stood for for the last twenty years in my mind, and the minds of my countrymen—the Bay of Pigs, Missile Crisis, Che, Angola, Ethiopia, Mariel Harbor—as I promenaded across the crowded hotel lobby, the afternoon sun slanting in across the polished stone floor, wearing camouflage fatigues, with Winchester-Western Super X 12-gauge shells rattling in the bellows pockets of my fatigue jacket, and with a camouflage-painted 870 Wingmaster pump laid with studied insouciance across my shoulder, *without* drawing a glance. The Cuban government had an obvious interest in seeing to it that American sportsmen visited the island and left behind their hard American currency, and were not tampered with in the process; but this seemed a case of taking politesse to the realm of the absurd.

While I was drinking one night with an official of the hotel in the Hotel Morón's lightless disco, a white-jacketed waiter materialized at my shoulder and presented me with some baffling document to sign regarding, I believe, my exchange of U.S. dollars, several rounds of drinks, and a peroxide blonde. When I examined the thing by matchlight and still could not fathom its purpose, the official leaned across the table and shouted the explanation into my ear, above the music, "It so nobody *fuck* with your!" As he sat back, grinning proudly at his command of that most essential English, I saw no choice but to stroke the pen across *la cuenta* with a magnanimous flourish. And fuck with mine absolutely no one did while I was in Cuba, anti-Americanism being confined for the most part to official displays on posters and in government publications and in massive red-flagged parades around the Plaza de la Revolución back in Havana.

If the average Cuban had one complaint against the United States, in fact (in those pre-Grenada days), it would have been for what he perceived to be the purely punitive trade embargo that had succeeded in creating the most spectacular collection of vintage fifties Detroit autos to be seen on the streets of any nation. Grandly finned Dodge Furies, De Sotos held together by three hundred coats of paint and a Crusonian ingenuity, '57 Chevies that could still break the heart of Saturday night, all passed in stately navigation around Morón's plaza square. New cars, government-issued Russian makes and Fiats, were said to be quite reasonably priced, but were rarities that tended to find their ways into the garages of doctors, professors, and politicos. For an everyday Cuban, on the other hand, a '54 Buick Sedan purchased from the original owner might represent an investment in the neighborhood of ten thousand pesos, with the official exchange rate in Cuba running at $1.30 (U.S.) to the peso.

In the People's Republic, then, our afternoons were for duck hunting. We would travel by bus with our guns and shells out to the Base Náutica on the Laguna where we would board a 62-foot diesel cruiser and with our guides cross the choppy water. With us would be the American tour agency's representative, Steve Shoulders, a Texan by birth, a robust and bearded fellow who spent much of his year in Cuba with his beautiful Cuban wife, looking after American hunters and fishermen who had come south. And with us also would be Mariño.

Mariño was tall and thin, eternally smiling, the retired personnel manager of a sugar mill, and what he did not know about hunting in Ciego de Ávila province was not worth knowing. He was almost sixty, wore old tennis shoes, and walked with long springing strides an unconscionable number of miles through mangrove swamps or around milo fields in the course of a day. Men half his age had tried to keep pace with him and barely lived to regret it. One time during duck season, the story went, he had led a young Cuban, who wished to learn the art of guiding American sportsmen, on a peppy little shakedown jaunt through the swamp to test his mettle. Pausing periodically to allow the much younger man to catch up, Mariño would take an occasional shot at a teal or wood duck slipping through the trees. He would then slip the dead bird's head through a leather strap tied to his belt, letting the bird hang down along his leg. Once when the young man slogged his way up to him, he reported to Mariño of having heard something "back there" among the trees.

Crocodile, Mariño assured him.

Crocodile? the young man squeaked.

Yes, but only the females during the nesting season were really dangerous.

And, uh, the nesting season . . . ? the young man just hated to ask.

Oh, Mariño supposed, right about now. But only if there were some blood in the water, or the like, would there be any risk of an attack, he further explained, turning to continue on through the knee-deep water, a red billow trailing behind him as he towed along his raft of dead ducks.

After half an hour of travel on the Laguna in the afternoons our big boat would turn and make its way through a narrow gut between two reefs, the channel marked by long sticks driven into the mud of the lagoon bottom. On rare early morning hunts, or at night on the way out, a jolly boat would have to be sent ahead to

mark this passage with a light or the big boat would run aground—
and sometimes did anyway. Now, though, we could make straight
through the gut for the edge of the mangrove forest surrounding the
lagoon and anchor just outside it. Transferring to the jolly boat, we
would bounce across the chop, the salt water misting over us in a
fine spray.

The jolly boat's motor would slow as we drew up to the
mangroves, and we would perceive then the long tunnel that had
been cut and dug out of the dense green tangle. We would churn
slowly through this tunnel's oily-looking water, listening to the
sounds of unseen jungle birds, until we came to a bank where the
small flat-bottomed hunting boats, the sort the Cubans called
chalanas, would be stacked and waiting. The boats would be placed
in the water and the hunters and guides would pair off, each of us
hunters, with his guide poling, moving in his boat into a smaller,
shallow inner lagoon of brackish water with isolated mangrove trees
scattered out in it. Every few yards as we traveled, the *chalana*
would skid up onto a submerged snag, the guide grunting, *"Muchos
truncos,"* as he heaved us off and then drove his wooden pole into the
mud again, propelling us on.

By now it would be late afternoon, and the heat of the glowing
tropical sun in the windless lagoon would press on our backs like a
great hand. Then the sweating guide would pole us into the cool
shade under one of the lagoon's mangroves, and I would look up to
find a handmade ladder rising up to a railed wooden shooting
platform built far up in the tree's branches.

After I'd ascend into the stand with my Wingmaster and
shells, the guide would pole back out and chuck his rather weary-
looking bunch of decoys onto the water—the only rules of decoy
placement in Cuba, where the very idea of decoys for ducks brought
on something like acute risibility in the Cubans, seeming to be a
loose set in the morning and a tight set in the afternoon, somewhere
where the shooter would not have to look directly into the rising or
setting sun, and with perhaps just the barest of ripples to give the
dekes some action and lend credibility to the subterfuge. The dekes
thus placed according to afternoon rules, the guide would pole the

chalana back under the mangrove, tie her off to the ladder, then climb up a few rungs himself and sit and light a smoke, waiting along with me for the birds to fly.

It was not until after the sun had gone down, however, that the birds would really fly. You would see them then, large flights coming into the lagoon for the night, silhouetted against the twilight. While you waited for them during the afternoon, though, you would watch some herons, very white, feeding off in a shaded corner of the lagoon, or watch a flight of black skimmers passing near you, their bodies inches above the water, their long bills ripping it like scissors tearing a sheet of satin.

At times in the afternoon you could hear Mariño as he made his way around the perimeter of the lagoon, a section or more in area, hooting and firing off his *escopeta* to drive any birds already on the water or the roost back into the air. Sometimes he would emerge from the mangrove forest to wade across the lagoon, and if he passed near your stand he would pause to lift the duck hanging from his leather strap and spread open the feathers to show you.

"Blue. Wing," he would pronounce in the only English I can ever remember hearing him use, smiling like the Bodhisattva of pass shooting.

Very often Mariño's walking in the mangroves did send up flights of ducks, and as you saw them coming in, you would squat down in your stand behind the branches' green leaves, your guide looking up expectantly. The ducks would come in extremely low and at high speeds, merely dipping a wing toward the decoys in salute, and you would find yourself shooting *down* at them as they passed, your shot string pearling the water a good yard or two behind them. This would be of invaluable assistance to your *next* shot, of course, letting you know how much to pick up your lead when another skein of ducks skidded by under your stand, and enabling you, with luck, to make a nice double on Bahama pintails—one cartwheeling into the water as the other dropped with his wings down and his head thrown back, both of them drakes with bloodred patches of color on their bills.

Also in the late afternoon you might get a high shot at the large white-crowned pigeons coming over on their way to their roosts, but it was not until last light that the ducks—and mostly woodies at that—would put in a serious appearance. The air by then would be thick with mosquitoes and a little *pinche* bastard that could not be seen or felt—but if he made it past your repellent and got to your skin, late at night as you lay in your bed in the hotel, listening to the band playing below in the courtyard by the pool, your ankles and wrists would begin to feel as if they were blazing with a candescent heat from his bites, sending you padding off into the bathroom to run cold tap water over them for twenty minutes and only temporarily slacken the pain. At last light in your stand you could literally breathe in a vapor of such insects, but it would not matter in the slightest as the black shapes of ducks began hurtling across the sky.

I would shoot three-quarters of my birds in that last half-hour before nightfall. Not a few I would take at eye level as they were coming right at me. It gave me pause to wonder if some dying wood duck, in all All-Star Tribute to Irony, was going to sail on into my head and crack my skull into pieces like the white shards of a shattered coffee cup.

As my guide would pole out to retrieve a downed bird, I would invariably drop one or two or three more on all sides of my stand and have to direct him to the marks in my scrambled Spanish. Finally would come the time when the next duck I shot would be the one neither of us could find. I would call the guide in then.

We would pole back under the warm stars, the ducks laid out in the bow *precisely* like a row of feathered mandolins. I would slap at a mosquito on my neck, then lift a woodie to turn it over in my hand as the boat sighed across the water. We would reenter the mangrove tunnel and the stars would be gone and the guide would call the darkness " '*Scuro*," in a whisper.

In February, in the spawning season, as we rode back out to the cruiser in the jolly boat, the water of the tunnel would be filled with pulsing green animal lights, the stars below us now. Then there would come into view the bright lights of the cruiser at anchor, highlighting the pitch and toss of the large lagoon's surface as we drew across it to the cruiser's stern. On board the big boat would be waiting rum and ice and cold fresh lobster in a Hollandaise sauce made with eggs bartered from an old black man who lived alone on an island out in the Laguna where he made charcoal—no one on board able, or willing, to venture an opinion as to exactly what *manner* of eggs we were enjoying. As we made our way back across the dark water to the dock, we would sip rum while watching on the land the fiery lights of the harvested cane fields as they burned into the night.

Mornings in Cuba were for dove. The shooting would come not right at first light but usually after the sun was well risen. The shooting was over that cut rice field, and it would draw in flights of mourning dove in numbers better suited to astronomy than to natural history. It was not a little daunting, with your bird boy squatting beside you, pointing at this gray swarm and shouting, "¡Ahí, ahí!"—in the same lyric way I remembered the Turkana gun bearer in Kenya pointing up at an incoming flight of sand grouse and shouting, "N'dio, n'dio!"—to rise up and empty your 12 gauge of all the Italian low-brass 9s you were now shooting and not hit a thing. The difficulty, you see, with *so* many birds in a single wad was trying to select which one to shoot. It seemed that just when you would lock onto a dove, he'd perform some kind of barrel roll or an Immelmann turn—lacking only a colored smoke trail and a pylon to loop around to make his act complete—and you would end up blowing out a chunk of blue sky.

"O," your bird boy in his camo shirt and billed cap with adjustable plastic tabs on the back and the name of an Indiana coal company printed on the crown would say softly.

My lifetime batting average on mourning dove stands around .370, but I would not begin to make up on it until later in the morning when the birds had thinned out enough to cease looking like a blizzard of Valenzuela screwballs and began flying straight and strong in singles and pairs and triples. Then they would begin to fall and my bird boy would be up and running through the yellow rice stubble after them. I can't remember him ever losing one, either.

One morning I killed more dove than I had ever killed in a single day in my life before. I went through two hundred shotgun shells before noon and was still well shy of the limit. That's when I handed my shotgun to my bird boy and let him shoot. He shot quite deftly, considering that hunting is a great luxury for the Cubans, though an enthusiastically, and often illicitly, pursued one. As he shot—and when I wasn't retrieving his birds for *him* in what I suppose could be interpreted as a show of solidarity with the workers—I went through the pile of dove, holding them up, turning them over in my hand, examining their violet-gray plumage. There was a monumental pile of dead dove there, and maybe I should have even felt bad about killing them all, but I didn't. I felt merely spent, taxed, the sport having been transmuted into a task. At dinner that night in the hotel, though, when the heaped platters of fresh dove breasts, broiled under strips of bacon, were brought to the table and my friend and I created another pile of dead dove, this one of bones stripped clean of their dark, wild flesh, that particular task did seem well rewarded.

Even so, I now have trouble remembering more than a few of the shots I made on all those mourning doves that morning, while I have no trouble whatsoever in recalling the shots I made on the two white-winged doves I killed another morning in Cuba—on the *only* two whitewings I have ever killed. I was standing at the edge of a milo field, hearing Mariño circling it, clapping and hooting to keep the dove airborne. I saw the pair of birds coming a long way off. Recognizing them instantly as whitewings, I hunkered down into the milo and hoped they would hold to their course, which would carry them over me. They did not vary in their flight, and as they swept over me I rose up and made a perfect double. The bird boy brought them to me, and I studied these two birds with care, wanting the first two of my life always to remain in my memory.

Half again as large as mourning doves, these whitewings, still bright with color so soon after death, had violet heads with shallow-water-turquoise flesh showing around their open eyes. A little ways below each eye was a spot of deep blue feathers. Farther down on their necks the feathers had a coppery sheen to them, and there was a grayish purple cast to their bellies. The primary feathers were black, and two clean white stripes ran along the upper wings. The tail was reddish brown with white on the edges, the feet dark red, and the beak long and black and polished. What had Emerson, or *somebody,* called his young son, a "domesticated sunbeam"? Well, here we had two unique feathered segments of the rainbow. I hefted them, one in each hand, and grinned at the bird boy.

When I didn't shoot, I'd fish for largemouth bass in Lake Redonda. From my bass boat I would flip a Mr. Twister plastic worm up into the roots of the green mangroves and gently bounce it back out to me across the mossy bottom. It was the smaller bass, the three- and four-pounders, who always seemed to put up the more spirited fight, thrashing and running and making a jump once in a while. Reeling in a big fish often seemed like leading a tired horse into a corral. Sometimes, though, a real "hawg," in the language of bass fishermen, maybe ten pounds or better for all I knew, would take the worm and drive off with it into the mangrove thicket as if I were standing in the Morón town plaza on a warm Saturday afternoon, smoking a three-peso Montecristo cigar and wearing a crisp white *guayabera* shirt, and making an accomplished cast with my Fenwick graphite rod and my Ambassadeur 5000 bait-casting reel, sank the barbed hook into the rusting chrome bumper of one of the parading Chevies. All you could do then was let it go until the line parted. Then wait quietly for the bar boat to run out from the dock across the green water and the bartender on board to mix you swiftly a tall icy *mojito* with crushed minty yerba buena leaves floating in it. And no doubt quite unfairly, I found this Mr. Twister bassin' to be, to my tastes, a resolutely numb-nuts game.

One afternoon, therefore, to get away from it, my fishing guide and I ran out to one of the channels off Redonda that opened onto the sea, hunting tarpon. In a weedy stretch of water by the channel's bank I saw the sleek fuselages of some of those outsize herring rolling. Tying a shock tippet, I tried throwing a plug at their wakes when they rolled. Then, tying on some tobacco-colored wire leader, I tried a dead fish, a small palometa, on a big silver hook. Yet even when that didn't succeed, I still knew there was something in this fishing for tarpon that could bring me back to Cuba someday.

Bring me back . . .

The local variation on the flu hit me when I was in Cuba. It was a minor ailment, no more, really, than a few days of disorientation and angst, accompanied by night sweats. After dinner I would wait politely for the fever in the hotel bar, drinking rum and listening to the bartender in the white shirt and black tie, his hair the color of milled steel, his jowls quivering, tell me about the old days in Havana when drinks would be christened for Mary Pickford—"a great *artiste,*" the barkeep would assure me. On top of the stainless-steel refrigerator behind him sat a good bass mounted red-gilled on a piece of driftwood with bottles of *ron* and whiskey and Soviet pepper vodka arrayed in front of it. Leaning on the bar, he would tick off on his fingers for me the batting order of the great St. Louis *Cardinales* of 1933 as I poured more straight Havana Club into my cocktail glass.

"Leo Durocher," he would intone. "Dizzy Dean."

With burlesqued paranoia, the bartender would quickly search the room for spies and informers, then slide his plump hand across the bar and grasp my cocktail glass by its stem. Raising it, he would adroitly flip the rum down his hatch, the gesture in its way probably not unlike the great Dean's as he picked up a slow roller back to the mound and flipped it to first. The bartender would smile Cheshirely as he set the empty glass down. Then the fever would arrive and wash over me in a heated wave.

Back in my room that smelled overpoweringly of insecticide and air conditioning, I would lie on my dorm bed and listen to the band in the courtyard strike up a Kenny Rogers hit, sung in English, while the many Cubans in attendance would dance the steps of American dances, wearing American boots and jeans and cowboy hats—gotten ahold of *somehow*—maybe even dreaming American dreams—or at least dreams of Miami. Then the music would switch to something disco—Afro-Cuban rhythms shipped north to be powdered and sintered and homogenized before running the embargo back south again. The only chances I had in Cuba for hearing real Cuban music, and tasting real Cuban food (the hotel fare being simulated American commissary cuisine), came on my last Saturdays in Ciego de Ávila province when we would have a farewell picnic in a grove of broad-leafed banana trees by the shore of Redonda. We'd be served an entire barbecued pig, black beans and rice, boiled *yuca,* sweating bottles of Hatuey beer, and dishes of the richest ice cream yet concocted by the hand of man, while a local band of black and mulatto men in simple clothes played hot merengue licks on guitars and brass and a big stand-up bass.

If on my last Saturday night in Cuba the fever subsided, I would go to the hotel's private lightless disco and buy my fishing guide and his *novia* for the evening a bottle of rum, which because I was a tourist cost me only four pesos, but would have cost my guide, because he was not, twenty-five. After the bottle came and we shared a drink, I would excuse myself and make my way across the packed dance floor, the laboring air conditioner trying valiantly to lay an arctic wind across it, to another table spread with a white cloth. I would talk with the Cuban girl sitting there, the one who spoke English and for some reason found my jokes funny—"You are, eh, *muy cómico.*" We would dance; and when the waiter came to the table again to ask me if I would have another drink, I would decline.

There would be a DC-3 waiting for me on Sunday morning in Camagüey, the girl and I both knew as we left the disco at midnight and walked slowly across the courtyard back to the hotel lobby, skirting the other band and dancers out by the pool. In the warm night I could smell the cane fields burning. Old Mariño, *Mariño viejo,* made his evening constitutional at just such times as this, I also knew, traveling over wide sweeps of the countryside, stepping briskly mile after mile. Perhaps he is, I thought, at this moment on the move.

Inside the hotel the girl and I rode up in the elevator together. At the girl's floor the operator held the door and watched us as we shook hands properly in the hallway and promised to meet again when I returned. But that is not a simple proposition anymore. There is no handy way to reach there now and I must wait here, trying to understand what it is I miss and what I do mean by *Cuba.*

Acknowledgments

The list of those whose help and encouragement over the years have contributed to my writing is a long one: Tom Paugh and the other editors of *Sports Afield* magazine, in which most of the essays in this book first appeared; John Rechy of Los Angeles; F. Smith Fussner and Robert Peterson of Portland, Oregon; Thomas McCambridge of Santa Monica, California; Paul Merzig of Chicago; Robert J. McIntyre of Austin, Texas; Edward Ehre of Sarasota, Florida; Roy Cooper of Downey, California; the late Millie Owen and Elaine Chubb, the copy editors; and William Doerflinger, my editor at E. P. Dutton, Inc. To all these people I wish to express my sincere gratitude.

T.M.